WORLD LEADERSHIP IN THE BALANCE

China and the US Clash for Supremacy

D0869172

WORLD LEADERSHIP IN THE BALANCE

China and the US Clash for Supremacy

Pierre-Antoine Donnet

Translated by Richard Lein

World Scientific

NEW JERSEY · LONDON · SINGAPORE · BEIJING · SHANGHAI · HONG KONG · TAIPEI · CHENNAI · TOKYO

Published by

World Scientific Publishing Co. Pte. Ltd.
5 Toh Tuck Link, Singapore 596224
USA office: 27 Warren Street, Suite 401-402, Hackensack, NJ 07601
UK office: 57 Shelton Street, Covent Garden, London WC2H 9HE

Library of Congress Cataloging-in-Publication Data
Names: Donnet, Pierre-Antoine, author.
Title: World leadership in the balance : China and the US clash for supremacy /
    Pierre-Antoine Donnet ; Translated by: Richard Lein.
Description: Hackensack, NJ : World Scientific, [2021] | Includes bibliographical references.
Identifiers: LCCN 2021012989 | ISBN 9789811235047 (hardcover) |
    ISBN 9789811236211 (paperback) | ISBN 9789811235054 (ebook for institutions) |
    ISBN 9789811235061 (ebook for individuals)
Subjects: LCSH: China--Foreign economic relations--United States. |
    United States--Foreign economic relations--China. | China--Commerce--United States. |
    United States--Commerce--China.
Classification: LCC HF1604.Z4 U63913 2021 | DDC 337.51073--dc23
LC record available at https://lccn.loc.gov/2021012989

British Library Cataloguing-in-Publication Data
A catalogue record for this book is available from the British Library.

For any available supplementary material, please visit
https://www.worldscientific.com/worldscibooks/10.1142/12233#t=suppl

Desk Editor: Aanand Jayaraman

Typeset by Stallion Press
Email: enquiries@stallionpress.com

This book is dedicated to Paul Jean-Ortiz, the foreign policy advisor of French President François Hollande. Jean-Ortiz was a China expert and organizer of Operation Yellowbird to help Chinese dissidents who participated in the Tiananmen Square protests of 1989. He died prematurely on July 31, 2013.

Foreword
Courage and Loyalty

I have known Pierre-Antoine Donnet since 1991, the year I became his editor at the Le Seuil publishing house, and I immediately appreciated the young writer and journalist. He had already published, at Gallimard, *Tibet mort ou vif* (*Tibet Dead or Alive*), a book pleading for support for Tibet in its confrontation with Chinese colonialism. I quickly guessed that he was in love with Asia. I associated him instinctively in my mind with a much older colleague whom I admired a lot, Robert Guillain, who lived almost forty years in *The Far East*, to use the title of his memoir.[1]

All the more so since the manuscript that Donnet had brought me, *Le Japon achète le monde* (*Japan Buys the World*), also reminded me of Guillain, a man who was viewed in Japan, until his death in 1998, as something like a precious friend and connoisseur of their culture. But as Guillain had known Japan in pain and tragedy (incendiary bombardments of Tokyo by American B-29s, Hiroshima, Nagasaki, etc.), Donnet wove a portrait of a Japan that had become extremely wealthy, able to conquer the world not by arms but by its technological ingenuity and commercial skills.

Donnet knows what he is talking about. He had been appointed, from 1993 to 1999, as a correspondent for Agence France-Presse in Tokyo. But that is not all: I noticed in this agency journalist a rigorous concern for exact, complete, cross-checked information. It gave value

---

[1] Robert Guillain, *Orient Extrême, une vie en Asie,* Paris, Seuil, 1968.

to his analyses and his points of view. To these virtues I add another that is rarer than one might imagine: the ability to rise above, to assess the situation and fate of a country from a global perspective. So I was not surprised when he brought me a larger work in 1998: *Le Choc Europe/Asie* (*The Europe-Asia Clash*), also published at Le Seuil in its contemporary history collection.

I will add that he was a great help to me when I encouraged my friend Cabu (murdered by jihadists with his colleagues at *Charlie Hebdo* on January 7, 2015) to pursue a magnificent effort: to make graphic books about countries. These books gradually formed a sort of collection. The drawings in these books had to be accompanied by an explanatory text, in effect making them two books in one. Pierre-Antoine Donnet agreed to write the text for *Cabu au Japon* (*Cabu in Japan*) in 1993, *Cabu en Chine* (*Cabu in China*) in 2000, then for *Cabu en Inde* (*Cabu in India*) in 2002, works which found their mark. They would not have been possible without Pierre-Antoine.

And now, 20 years later, I find him displaying the same qualities, enriched and deepened by experience, in the book that you will read here. It is about the global competition between Donald Trump's United States and Xi Jinping's China. That is, between a superpower in political crisis (the USA) and a China that aspires to steal world leadership from the Americans. This rivalry of two giants will certainly dominate the years, if not decades, to come. Filled with the courage of an observer, the attentive accuracy of a journalist and the clarity of expression of a talented writer, here is a book which is making its appearance at the best possible time.

Jean-Claude Guillebaud
Writer, Essayist, Lecturer, Editor and Journalist

Preface

A major event has taken place since the publication of the French version of this book: the election on November 3 of Joe Biden as the 46th president of the United States. Once installed in the Oval Office, one of the first foreign policy issues he will have to confront will be China. No 180-degree turn in US policy is expected here: Biden intends to maintain a tough policy against Beijing. Democrats, like the Republicans, believe it is imperative to "contain" the rapid rise onto the world stage of a country that — to their eyes — represents a threat to US national security.

All that we can expect is a change in rhetoric. Joe Biden will abstain from speaking of the "China virus" and is likely to adopt more measured language towards China and its leaders. His pick for secretary of state, Anthony Blinken, will unlikely target the Chinese Communist Party as has Mike Pompeo, who spoke of it as "the primary challenge today in the free world". Remarks Blinken made in January just after his confirmation, bear this out. "It's not a secret that the relationship between the United States and China is arguably the most important relationship that we have in the world going forward," Blinken told reporters. "It's going to shape a lot of the future that — that we all live, and increasingly that relationship has some adversarial aspects to it. It has competitive ones. And it also still has cooperative ones," he said. Biden has also promised to consult America's European allies on whether or not to pursue the commercial and technological sanctions that Trump has imposed upon China.

Among the first measures that Joe Biden has promised to take after being sworn into office on January 20, 2021, is to rejoin the Paris Agreement on climate change and the World Health Organization (WHO). Biden is likely to adopt a foreign policy, apart from China, that is a complete departure from his predecessor. Whereas Donald Trump used his four-year mandate to pursue a largely isolationist policy that gave China an open road to increase its influence in international organizations, Biden has signaled he intends for the US to return to a more active role. "America is back, to lead the world, not retreat from it," he said in late November when outlining some of his personnel choices. That may not necessarily lead to more tensions with China. "Democrats appear less militant, so they may take more care to prevent even limited military conflicts and pay more attention to crisis management communication with China," Shi Yinhong, a professor of international relations and director of the Centre on American Studies at Renmin University of China, told AP shortly before election day.

One of the most delicate issues that awaits Joe Biden is China's increasingly belligerent posture in the South China Sea and its attitude towards Taiwan, which is the most contentious issue between Beijing and Washington by far. At the least, Biden's policy "won't be as emotional and ridiculous as Trump's," said Yu Wanli, a professor of international relations at Beijing Language and Culture University. "Biden is a problem for China because his administration would likely stick China on human rights, and his declared approach of working with allies to constrain China could happen and would complicate China's advance," said Robert Sutter, a China expert at George Washington University. An indication of Biden's approach to the Taiwan issue was gleaned from an article he wrote for New York-based Chinese-language newspaper *World Journal*, published two weeks before the election, in which he promised to rebuild relationships with Washington's closest partners in the Pacific. "That includes deepening our ties with Taiwan, a leading democracy, major economy, technology powerhouse — and a shining example of how an open society can effectively contain Covid-19," Biden wrote.

In an opinion piece published in the French daily *Le Monde* on November 17, French Foreign Minister Yves Le Drian and his German counterpart Heiko Maas called the election of Joe Biden an opportunity to renew transatlantic ties to better confront China. "We know that under the Biden administration, China will remain a focal point of US foreign policy. For us, [China] is at once a partner, a competitor and a systemic rival. We therefore have an interest in making a common front to respond to its rising power with pragmatism, while at the same time conserving channels of cooperation which are necessary to confront, with Beijing, the global challenges of the Covid-19 pandemic and climate change," they wrote.

Thus, we see that irrespective of any change of style by their leaders, the substance of the rivalry between China and the United States remains and will likely define the contours of their relations for many years to come. That is because the Americans can't imagine for a moment ceding their hegemonic status to China. There is no question of leaving open the possibility for the apprentice to supplant the master. A Democrat in the White House probably stands more of a chance of convincing European partners to adopt a joint approach against China. There is certainly an opening to exploit by the European Union, which has been very cold to the rhetoric and posturing of Mike Pompeo, but which in recent months has clearly been adopting a harder line against China.

If Donald Trump viewed relations with China as transactional through a prism of economic advantage and commercial deals, it is clear that Joe Biden will focus more — and likely be intransigent — upon human rights issues. Beijing will prickle at the spotlight being placed upon its treatment of the Uighurs in Xinjiang, the fate of Tibet and Hong Kong, and a renewed focus by the West on universal human values. Biden pledged if elected he would meet with the Dalai Lama, the Tibetan spiritual leader that Beijing considers to be a "dangerous separatist".

Even if they would never admit it publicly, the Chinese regime clearly favored Joe Biden. China may have profited from Donald Trump's isolationist streak to secure more leadership roles in international institutions. However, Beijing was horrified by his unpredictability and clearly wanted to dial back tensions. "Reversing the old cliche, they'd prefer the devil they don't know to the devil they do know," said June Teufel Dreyer, a China expert at the University of Miami. Michael Carpenter, a key foreign policy adviser to Biden, said the new president-elect would unite Europe as "friends and allies" when it came to China. "Donald Trump's approach to China [was] a very narrow preoccupation with a trade deficit," Carpenter said. "What a Biden administration will do… is work together with our partners across the world to put up a united front and to end this systemic manipulation."

Beijing is not deceiving itself. In a report on its fifth plenum meeting at the end of October, the Chinese Communist Party underlined without stating explicitly that it does not expect a quick improvement in its relations with the United States. "The international environment is becoming more and more complex while instability and insecurity are rising significantly," the official communique said without mentioning the US elections. Uncharacteristically, the 6,000-character document uses the word "security" 22 times. The US elections drew the world's attention to a robust, if bumpy, democratic process, and also drew a sharp contrast to the frozen political environment in China under the autocratic grip of Xi Jinping. "My fellow Americans, yesterday, once again proved that democracy is the heartbeat of this nation… has been the heartbeat of this nation for two centuries," Biden said the day after the election. "And even in the face of pandemic, more Americans voted this election than ever before in American history. Over 150 million people cast their votes. I think that's just extraordinary. And if we had any doubts, we shouldn't have any longer, about a government of, by, and for the people." A beautiful demonstration of US democracy that thumbs its nose at the Communist China of Xi Jinping which has never held free elections.

Meudon, France
January 28, 2021

Acknowledgments

First of all, I would like to acknowledge my gratitude to Richard Lein who tackled with talent and in record time the translation of this book. It goes as well to World Scientific Publishing to take on this English edition. I would like to extend my heartfelt thanks to Mark O'Neill, without whose help this English version of my book would never have seen the light of day. Anthony Barker and Maurice Ralphs for kindly casting their attentive eyes over the English draft. I thank my son Pierre-Arnaud, who lives in Hong Kong, for his assistance in finding leads and precious sources in the complicated labyrinth of Chinese-American relations. My thanks also go to Agence France-Presse, to which I have devoted 37 years of my professional life and which has been an inexhaustible source of information for this book. I have a debt of gratitude to Manon Viard, editor at L'Aube publishing house, who immediately believed in my project. Finally, I owe a great debt to my wife, Monika, who accepted with good grace the numerous hours stolen from our daily life to write this book.

Contents

Introduction

China has experienced dizzying economic progress since the 1980s. It is now in the process of overtaking the United States to become the world's leading economic power. And it has ambitions to overtake America in the technological and scientific fields as well. While Beijing's Silk Roads project (Belt and Road Initiative) is less ambitious than initially envisaged due to the reservations of partner countries, it will nevertheless deepen China's market penetration in Asia, Africa and Europe. Meanwhile, the United States has finally come to the realization that China is now its main rival. The two countries engaged in trade negotiations in 2019 but nevertheless continued to exchange barbs against a backdrop of fierce competition. The difficulties encountered by Chinese telecommunications champion Huawei are emblematic of this unprecedented rivalry. But for the first time in forty years, communist China has been forced to sit down at the negotiation table. The reality is that China and the United States have entered a cold war, and tensions have only deepened further with the outbreak of the COVID-19 pandemic. While the United States remains by far the leading global military power, China has made major strides that already challenge the ability of Washington to effectively support its allies in the region. Moreover, China shows no sign of slowing its efforts to close technological gaps. It has made breathtaking progress in rolling out a high-speed rail network and developing civilian nuclear energy. China has also become the top producer of and market for battery electric vehicles, a leading player in mobile telephones and networks, and a pioneer in the development of artificial intelligence. To this list we can add recent progress in space exploration and we may expect similar advances in civil aviation.

The rivalry between China and the United States has turned into a conflict of civilizations. It pits a democracy whose decline is evident but which nevertheless remains vibrant and has demonstrated its ability to rebound, against a single-party dictatorship which seems to still be firmly in charge. There is an abyss between Americans who are jealous of their individual freedoms and their way of life — the *American way of life* — and the Chinese who are attached to their multi-millennial history and proud of their rapid economic development. But while most Chinese have escaped poverty, they remain under close surveillance by the state which increasingly uses technology to impose Orwellian-style social control and keep politics in a straitjacket. A permanent member of the UN Security Council, China has used its role as the workshop of the world to become the dominant economic power across much of the planet. And President Xi Jinping's "Chinese Dream" initiative intends to lead the country to first place in all key spheres by 2049, the 100th anniversary of the establishment of the People's Republic. China will have then finally expunged the humiliation of the Opium Wars. The Chinese derive a legitimate pride and never miss an opportunity to point out that their brilliant history spans more than five thousand years,[1] while young America can point to barely two and half centuries of existence. In November 2017, during US President Donald Trump's first state visit to China, Xi Jinping declared in front of Chinese television cameras: "We have 3,000 years with a written language." Trump replied: "I guess the older culture, they say, is Egypt with 8,000." Xi acknowledged that "Egypt is a bit more ancient. But the only continuous civilization to continue onwards is China." (Egypt is a bit more ancient, 2017)

Meanwhile, Europe is a helpless spectator in this frenzied race between one country which is striving to snatch world leadership from

---

[1] The discovery in 1936 of the ancient city of Liangzhu, now a UNESCO World Heritage Site, in the Yangtze River Delta, along with many artifacts including magnificent jade objects, attests to Chinese civilization stretching back 5,000 years.

another that has no intention of relinquishing the status it has held for a century. And old Europe is painfully aware that both are working to undermine its unity and its influence.

It should be remembered that China was the top power in the world for most of the last 20 centuries. Until the 18th century, when the Industrial Revolution began in the West, it was China that boasted the highest living standards on the planet. At the beginning of the Christian era, China accounted for more than a quarter of the world's wealth, but Europe was unaware of its existence. "The distances were enormous… and mutual ignorance was the norm," noted Hubert Testard (2019a), a specialist on Asia and international economic issues, on Asialyst.com.[2] In 1820, at the height of its power, China accounted for 36% of the world economy. What has passed before our eyes since 1979 can therefore be perceived by Chinese leaders as a just return to the situation before the humiliation inflicted upon it in the mid-nineteenth century by Western colonizers during the Opium Wars. The American economist and analyst David P. Goldman, a former Bank of America and Credit Suisse executive who is known for his column in *Asia Times Online* published under the pseudonym "Spengler", remarked that:

> China was the world's dominant manufacturing power for most of the last 1,000 years. Then it declined about 200 years ago at the beginning of the Industrial Revolution. The Chinese view this as a temporary aberration, and they want to re-establish China's preeminence. They look at Chinese technological dominance, both in terms of innovation and in control of major world markets, as the key to Chinese power and prosperity. (Gehriger, 2019)

Communist China started from far back. It should not be forgotten that in 1950 China was the poorest country in the world. Mao Zedong's reign was synonymous with great waves of famine and economic and political chaos. But following the economic reforms introduced by Deng Xiaoping beginning in 1979, China experienced three decades of annual GDP growth greater than 10%. Does the current slowdown reflect a crisis in the Chinese economic model? Opinions vary.

---

[2] Asialyst.com is a French website for analysis and news on Asia.

For some observers, China's model may have found its limit and is already suffering from trade tensions with the United States. For others, the current situation probably does not prefigure a deep crisis, but signals that changes are needed in the Chinese economy, which has been able to make easy gains from globalization over these past decades. In recent years, the People's Republic of China has become the top destination for international investments, ahead of the United States. In fact, since 2014 communist China has become the world's leading economic power in terms of GDP measured by purchasing power parity (PPP). It is also now the world's leading exporter. Between 1980 and 2007, China's GDP grew by a factor of 13! Certainly, economic growth has led to a significant increase in inequality and caused considerable damage to the environment. Beijing is today the fourth most polluted city in the world. But poverty has receded considerably. According to statistics published in the *OECD Observer* in September 2005, more than half of the reduction of absolute poverty in the world between 1980 and 2000 occurred in China. The poverty rate dropped from 97.5% in 1978 to 10.2% in 2012 then to 1.7% in 2018.[3] The Chinese government aimed to eliminate absolute poverty in 2020, including in rural areas, and thus create a "relatively prosperous society".

This performance was made possible by the economic reforms undertaken fifteen years after the end of the disastrous Cultural Revolution. They were accompanied by an impressive increase in the private sector. China has shifted from a Soviet-style planned economy to "socialism with Chinese characteristics". The private sector was responsible for 60% of the added value produced in 2018. In 2017, 90% of new jobs were created in the private sector. While the public sector remains powerful, it is also notoriously inefficient. The 90 largest state-owned enterprises drain more than half of public investment. Despite the rise in inequality, Chinese economic growth has allowed the emergence of a middle class that outnumbers that of the United States.

---

[3] Chinese National Bureau of Statistics.

On the other side of the Pacific, America has not lost much of what makes it outstanding. The awesome economic power of the United States continues to command respect throughout the world. In 2018 and 2019, the US economy remained dynamic, driven by solid domestic demand. Growth accelerated in 2018 (+3.0% as recorded by the Federal Reserve, after +2.5% in 2017), supported primarily by consumption and investment. Consumption remained robust thanks to the favorable situation in the labor market, which led to increasing disposable income, and tax cuts adopted as part of the 2017 tax reform. The fiscal stimulus adopted by Congress in March 2018 also contributed to supporting growth. The American economy basically hit full employment, with the unemployment rate falling to 3.5% in September 2019, its lowest level since December 1969! Job creation remained strong, however, with 136,000 jobs created that same month and an average of 220,000 jobs created per month in 2018. Meanwhile, inflation remained moderate: consumer price inflation stood at 1.9% in December 2018, close to the US Federal Reserve's target level. In October 2019, the US economy entered its 124th consecutive month of growth, the longest expansion recorded by the National Bureau of Economic Research (NBER) since 1854. "Some of the best Economic Numbers our Country has ever experienced are happening right now," Trump tweeted in September 2019.

Both the Chinese and US economies were, however, deeply affected by the coronavirus pandemic. The decade-long expansion in the US was brought to a halt with GDP falling by 4.8% in the first quarter of 2020. US industrial production fell 5.4% in March from February, according to Federal Reserve figures, the most severe drop since January 1946. The unemployment rate surged to 14.7% in April, its highest level since the 1930s, but quickly fell back under 10%. The pandemic is likely to leave its mark on the US economy for several years and many view it as having cost Trump reelection.

Meanwhile, the Chinese economy has also taken a hammering. GDP fell by 6.8% in the first quarter of 2020, when much of the country's economic activity was halted due to lockdowns, compared with the same period in 2019. It is the first contraction in Chinese

GDP since at least 1992, when official growth statistics began to be compiled. The drop was slightly worse than the 6.5% drop expected by analysts and followed the 6.0% growth registered in the final quarter of 2019. But China returned to growth in the second quarter with a 3.2% increase in GDP from the same period of 2019, according to China's National Bureau of Statistics, although some observers have doubts about the reliability of these encouraging figures.

Beyond this economic dashboard of the two leading economic powers on the planet, this book deals with the bitter competition that the two giants are engaged in today to keep or win world leadership. This relentless struggle for influence and political competition has given birth to a new cold war that has left Europe sidelined, bogged down in its endless internal differences. The world of tomorrow will witness a further intensification of this multifaceted rivalry between the two great powers. While America' hegemony was arousing mistrust and opposition throughout the world, China's new economic and technological imperialism has crossed borders to conquer places far from Beijing.

This struggle for world leadership is seen by many as a fundamental clash of civilizations. This is a view that Chinese President Xi Jinping publicly rejects, however. "If someone thinks their own race and civilization is superior and insists on remolding or replacing other civilizations, it would be a stupid idea and disastrous act," Xi told the Conference on Dialogue of Asian Civilizations in May 2019. (Zhen and Ng, 2019) But for French journalist Claude Leblanc, "the fear of seeing a non-Western country taking over global leadership encourages Americans to envisage a long-term confrontation with the Chinese." (Leblanc, 2019) A senior US State Department official has also explicitly linked the threat that China poses to the United States to race. Kiron Skinner, then director of policy planning at the US State Department, told a forum on US national security policy in April 2019 that "it's the first time that we will have a great power competitor that is not Caucasian." (Chan, 2019) "This is a fight with a really different civilization, and a different ideology, and the United States hasn't had that before," Skinner added. (*ibid.*)

So should we not conclude that there is today, on one side, an America which continues to stand as a bulwark for freedom in the world, and on the other, an authoritarian communist system which has, little by little, seduced certain emerging countries suspicious of the virtues of Western democracy? Perhaps, but not before looking one by one at all of the aspects — political, sociological, economic, military and technological — that will help us trace the outlines of this great conflict of the twenty-first century. There may not yet be a definitive answer to the question of whether the "American century" will be succeeded by the "Chinese century", whether we should expect Chinese domination to supplant American hyperpower. Nevertheless, by reflecting on these questions we gain greater insight into the changes taking place that will define our world for decades to come.

This book is the work of a journalist and not that of a researcher who specializes on China. It cannot, therefore, compete with the knowledge of an expert on that country. I did spend eight years of my life in the region at a pivotal moment in its political development, including my stays in Taiwan and Hong Kong to learn Chinese and my years in Beijing as a correspondent for Agence France-Presse. I have returned many times since. I have many dear friends there. As for the United States, I worked there for two years as an AFP correspondent accredited to the UN in New York. I conducted my investigation for this book methodically on a daily basis, checking my information from a multitude of first-hand sources, although I admit it has been pushed along by the intense flow of developments. I set myself the task of presenting here an honest picture that is as balanced as possible of a reality that will undoubtedly influence the future of the world, always keeping in mind the maxim dear to Deng Xiaoping about the need to "seek truth from facts".

Chapter 1

Democracy in the Face of Dictatorship

The Chinese Communist Party appears to be firmly anchored at the head of a one-party regime and does not seem ready to tolerate democratization. Individual freedoms are few in a country where the Party alone imposes the political rules. On the other side of the Pacific, American democracy hardly inspires the world anymore and is no longer the envied model it was at the end of World War II. Meanwhile, China is expanding its influence throughout the world and hopes to export its own political and social model to developing countries where elites do not trust a Western-type democratic system. The two models are hurtling towards a head-on collision. America continues to show off its banner of freedom, while the leaders of China, the last great communist country on the planet, reject the universal founding values of the United Nations. Meanwhile, the European Union remains the proverbial fifth wheel.

"Right and law are two forces; from their agreement is born order, from their antagonism is born disaster."

Victor Hugo [1802–1885]

Actes et paroles (*Deeds and Words*)

Volume I, 1876

In his controversial 1997 book *The Clash of Civilizations*, Harvard University professor Samuel Huntington argues that Confucian and Western civilizations are radically antagonistic on fundamental points.

A member of the National Security Council when Jimmy Carter was in the White House, Huntington notes that Confucian cultures value authority, hierarchy, the importance of consensus and the preeminence of power over individual freedoms. This differs radically from the American vision of society where primacy is placed on freedom, equality, democracy, individualism and human rights. "There are not two suns in the sky, nor two sovereigns over the people," said Confucius. This emphasizes the principle that harmony from hierarchy takes precedence over individual freedom, and both are subject to the primacy of the authority of the supreme leader. This Confucian principle may lead current Chinese leaders to conclude that there is no room in the world for two number ones: the United States and China. Order constitutes the supreme political value. Without order, chaos reigns. In this vision of the world and of society, freedom, in the American sense of the term, only upsets the hierarchy and leads to chaos.[1]

For Americans, on the contrary, democracy is the only legitimate form of government. The twenty-sixth American president, Theodore Roosevelt, who held office from 1901 to 1909, believed that the United States' mission was to spread American power, built on the notion of a universal civilization applicable to all human beings, all over the world. Maya Kandel, a researcher at the Sorbonne in Paris and an expert in the history of the United States, believes that "American exceptionalism" has a double meaning:

> It expresses, on the one hand, the identity of the country, the notion of a people achieving a unique and universal destiny on the promised land of the North American continent [and, on the other hand, defines] American foreign policy as a mission based on the conviction of a unique and special role entrusted to the country because it is the most qualified to guide the world

---

[1] The Chinese Communist leadership is also inspired by the thought of the legalist administrators who wielded power in China from the 8th century BC until the end of the Warring States period (3rd century BC) and who affirmed that "the prince must exercise power through tyranny, police, privation and for the exclusive sake of a centralized power, the spirit having no other ambition than to faithfully justify the raison d'état." (Étiemble, 1958: 53)

towards global peace and prosperity, because of what the United States is, or at least thinks it is: a country defined by a process of abundance that offers the achievement of a material "happiness" as promised in the Constitution, all dependent upon a model supposedly transferable and reproducible by everyone and everywhere in the world. (Kandel, 2018)

For the vast majority of Americans today, democratic rights and freedom are still considered universal values that should apply to the whole world.

The American and Chinese presidents, Donald Trump and Xi Jinping, nevertheless had one idea in common: they both aspired to make their country great, to paraphrase a Trump campaign slogan. But aside from that, they differed on everything. It is worth recalling to what extent the United States and China are profoundly different culturally, socially and politically.

A brief historical reminder. The United States entered the stage of world history in 1776 as the first modern democracy. Despite the practice of slavery which continued until the middle of the 19th century, the Revolution made America the first power of the modern world to enjoy a government that was authentically democratic: a government of the people, by the people and for the people. The 13 colonies, which declared their independence in 1776 and then formed a federation in 1787, represented the first nation of the modern world to have succeeded in combining the sovereignty of the people and government thanks to federalism. The United States was thus the first country to adopt a political system based on universal suffrage and freedom of expression. Tocqueville observed that "the social condition of the Americans is eminently democratic. It had this character from the birth of the colonies; it still has more nowadays." He adds: "The big advantage of Americans is to have achieved democracy without having to suffer from democratic revolutions, and to have been born equal instead of having become so." (Tocqueville, 2019 [1835]: 63) The United States continues to be governed by the oldest written constitution currently in force, drawn up in 1787–1788 for a country of four million inhabitants at the time. Founded on the principles of federalism, the limitation and separation of powers, and the freedom of citizens, the American political system has been extended from the 13 founding states, all located on the eastern seaboard, to the Pacific. It has enabled economic growth on a scale unprecedented in history. It has survived the political and social crises of the nineteenth century — especially the Civil War (1861–1865). It has opened the path for the United States to take on international responsibilities during the two World Wars and to its preeminence on the world stage from 1990.

Today, American democracy rests on the principle of a balance of power. The Constitution provides a separation of powers between the Presidency (the executive), the Supreme Court (the judiciary) and the Congress (the legislature with two chambers: the House of Representatives and the Senate). It is nevertheless a presidential system since the president is simultaneously the head of state, the head of the executive and the head of the armed forces. The presidency also plays an important role in legislative matters as it sets in part the legislative agenda of Congress and draws up the nation's budget. The Congress, however, remains very powerful. It does not always endorse the president's proposals and uses its oversight powers to investigate any and all subjects, sometimes causing difficulty for the chief executive. The consequences of World War II convinced Americans to defend and modernize their democratic practices. In the 1960s, the black minority finally attained in practice the right to vote that had been granted them nearly a century before. The principle of "one man, one vote" was finally achieved and the number of representatives truly became dependent upon the population of a constituency.

The low voter participation and the institutional crisis seen during the 2016 presidential election revealed an alienation from political life among many Americans and the existence of a moral crisis unprecedented in the country's history. And American-style democracy no longer seduces the world as much as it did at the end of World War II. The misdeeds of imperialism, the search for hegemony and the relative decline of the "beacon of mankind" have had their effect. Since the stinging setbacks of the Vietnam War (1963–1975) the American model has found its limits. Following the end of the Cold War, America redefined its political and military mission in what has been baptized the "Wolfowitz doctrine", which is to "to prevent the re-emergence of a new rival" and to discourage challenges to US leader-ship or those "seeking to overturn the established political and economic order." (Kandel, 2018) But the "acceptable hegemony" of the United States "presupposes a belief in the superiority of the American model: but it is this belief that has been undermined, not only in the world for the past few decades, but now and above all by a majority of Americans themselves for the first time in their history." (*ibid.*)

At the end of the twentieth century, US leaders "saw the unchecked power at their disposal as an opportunity to mold the international environment, and to reap even greater benefits in the future" accord-ing to Harvard University professor of international relations Stephen Walt. (Walt, 2006) "America's leaders have sought to persuade as many countries as possible to embrace their particular vision of a liberal-capitalist world order," he added. (*ibid.*) But many emerging nations are wary of the supposed virtues of democracy and liberalism. They often prefer an authoritarian regime. A demonstration of this mistrust occurred in the summer of 2019: on July 9 around 20 mostly Western countries sent a joint letter to the UN requesting China respond to accusations it had arbitrarily detained a million Uighurs in "re-education camps" in Xinjiang, the former East Turkestan. However, in response, 50 countries, including many Muslim coun-tries, expressed their support for China and its coercive action against the Uighurs.

The first direct encounter between China and the United States dates to 1849. Tens of thousands of Chinese disembarked in San Francisco as part of the gold rush. Fleeing from famine and dreaming of a better future in what they called in Chinese "the Mountain of Gold", these emigrants from southern China, who arrived on rickety wood ships, were quickly recognized as very good workers and employed in the construction of America's first transcontinental rail-road. But faced with the influx of Chinese immigrants, American newspapers quickly began to speak of a "yellow peril" and the authori-ties adopted the Chinese Exclusion Act in 1882.

Modern China was of course not always a communist dictatorship. On May 4, 1919, some 3,000 students demonstrated on Tiananmen Square in Beijing to protest against the Treaty of Versailles which delivered the eastern province of Shandong to Japan. Led by young progressive intellectuals, the students denounced stifling traditions, the power of the mandarins and the oppression of women. And they called for democracy. This May 4th Movement, which gave birth to Chinese nationalism, is commemorated by the communist regime even today. In 1911, after the fall of the imperial regime that had ruled China since 221 BC, the Republic of China was founded. It was a regime based on the Western idea of democracy that was heir to reformist and then revolutionary republican Chinese movements personified by Doctor Sun Yat-sen and his movement, the Kuomintang.

The Republic of China lasted until 1949, when the regime, corrupt and in the grip of a civil war against the Communists, withdrew to the island of Taiwan, where the Constitution of 1947 remains in effect. The defeat of the Kuomintang was in fact due considerably to the war waged against the invading Japanese forces from 1937. The Kuomintang lost more than 80% of its generals in the Sino-Japanese War, at a time when the Chinese Communist Party (CCP), holed up in mountain villages, saved its forces by rarely engaging the Japanese before passing onto the offensive against the Chinese nationalists whom it finally defeated in 1949. Taiwan still observes today the democratic orientations of the 1947 Constitution. The island of 24 million inhabitants is, in fact, the only living example of democracy in the Chinese world. Since the death in 1988 of President Chiang Ching-kuo, son of General Chiang Kai-shek, Taiwan has become deeply democratized. This vibrant polity is the antithesis of arguments by some "China experts" that democracy is foreign to the Chinese nation. A multiparty system has taken root on the island since martial law was lifted in July 1987. The first legislative elections using direct universal suffrage took place in December 1989, followed by the first free presidential election in March 1990.

In 1949, after decades of struggle against the occupying Japanese forces and the weakening Kuomintang army, Mao Zedong's communist forces succeeded in taking power. Mao Zedong proclaimed the founding of the People's Republic of China on October 1, 1949, in Tiananmen Square in Beijing. Since that date, the Communist Party, the sole party in power, has imposed its rule on the whole country, except Taiwan.

Article 1 of the Chinese Constitution states that "the People's Republic of China is a socialist state of popular democratic dictatorship." Strongly inspired by their Soviet advisers, the Chinese Communists put in place a five-year development plan for the years 1953–1957. In 1955–1956 they introduced collectivism. All private industrial companies were nationalized (although the former managers often remained in charge), and the same was true for commerce (except retail trade). In the countryside, peasants were forced to group into cooperatives (only 7% of families were members of cooperatives in 1954; this rose to 100% in 1956). This system facilitated the collection of taxes. In theory, it should have also allowed for better use of labor and agricultural equipment. It was also meant to change mentalities through the renunciation of individualism.

The reign of the CCP was solidified under the leadership of Mao Zedong by several political campaigns that turned out to be catastrophic. One such campaign was the "Great Leap Forward", a reform program from 1958 to 1961 that intended to accelerate economic development by increasing industrial and agricultural productivity. The stated objective of this policy was to catch up within fifteen years with the UK economy, then the world's third largest. But the Great Leap Forward turned out to be an economic disaster. The hoped-for results were not achieved, with crops left rotting in the fields or in any case insufficient. Meanwhile, local officials, out of fear, submitted to the Communist Party falsified agricultural production figures. China experienced a terrible famine: according to figures from Chinese journalist and historian Yang Jisheng who spent a dozen years investigating the subject, some 36 million people died of hunger as a direct consequence of the Great Leap Forward. "Several tens of millions of men disappeared like that, without a sound, without a sigh, in indifference or stupidity," victims of a totalitarian regime led by the tyrant Mao Zedong, wrote the former journalist at the official Xinhua News

Agency. (Yang, 2012) "It's an unprecedented tragedy in the history of mankind that in normal climatic conditions, in the absence of war and epidemic, tens of millions of people died of hunger and there was large-scale cannibalism," he added. (*ibid.*) Jasper Becker, a Beijing correspondent for *The Guardian* at the time I was there, estimated the death toll of this national disaster to be at least 30 million. (Becker, 1996)

The other big political campaign that also caused a terrible tragedy for the Chinese people was the Cultural Revolution, which ran from 1966 to 1976. Seeing his power slipping away, Mao Zedong mobilized the country's youth to overthrow his opponents. But the young red guards went well beyond the aims that had been set for them. Millions of people were subjected to popular criticism and collective torture sessions, often driven to suicide or put to death by frenzied crowds. The regime has never provided a precise toll of these two political movements that deeply traumatized a whole generation of Chinese.[2]

In 1979, the moment had come for radical change. Aware that China was falling behind in the world, Deng Xiaoping launched his "Four Modernizations" program covering the fields of agriculture, industry, science and technology, and national defense. He also introduced at the same time daring economic reforms with the extraordinary slogan "To be rich is glorious". "It doesn't matter whether a cat is black or white, so long as it catches mice it is a good cat," proclaimed the nation's new patriarch. The results of this ideological turning point towards "market socialism with Chinese characteristics" were not long in coming. Activity burst forth from below, setting China on a period of super-fast economic growth that has slowed down significantly but remains far above the global average. The country overcame its economic slump and underdevelopment to become the world's second-largest economic power in less than forty years.

But the regime continues to rely on the CCP and China remains officially communist. Even if China today has a largely capitalist-inspired economic system, in the political sphere the CCP does not

---

[2] Yang Jisheng has written a second book focused on the Cultural Revolution, a French translation of which will be published soon by Editions du Seuil.

tolerate the existence of other parties or have any desire for democracy. The Party currently has some 90 million members. In terms of longevity, at 70 years it is closing in on the Communist Party of the Soviet Union, which had lasted for 74 years before expiring in 1991. The leaders of the regime are not elected, because there is no election by universal suffrage. In the absence of the separation of executive, legislative and judicial powers, the PRC is a dictatorship. Although some timid steps have been made in the direction of political liberalization, the Party keeps effective control over the country. Universal suffrage at village-level elections, introduced by Deng Xiaoping as part of his openness policy, was to have been subsequently extended to a higher level, but this never happened.

The Standing Committee of the Central Political Bureau of the CCP, composed of seven members, is the supreme decision-making body. All dissent is systematically suppressed. Activists are thrown in jail and severely punished. It is impossible to forget the bloody repression of the Tiananmen Square student movement which resulted in several hundred, if not several thousand deaths on June 4, 1989. On that day the army, on the orders of Deng Xiaoping and Prime Minister Li Peng, opened fire on youths calling for more democracy. This episode clearly demarcated the limits of the policy of openness and demonstrated the willingness of the communist authorities to assassinate their country's youth to save their own skin and impose their rule. The other organs of state power are the National People's Congress (NPC), the President of the Republic and the State Council. The NPC is a simple rubber-stamp assembly with no real power. Votes are taken almost unanimously. Members of the State Council include the prime minister, a varying number of deputy prime ministers, five state councilors and 29 ministers and heads of committees of the State Council. Political control remains firmly in the hands of Party leaders, creating an almost total concentration of power. In autonomous regions such as Tibet, the head of the executive is a member of the dominant local ethnic group as was the practice in the Soviet Union, while the head of the regional Party apparatus is Han Chinese.

After reaching the apex of power in 2012, Xi Jinping revealed himself to be an authoritarian ruler. His reign has been accompanied by a clear hardening of the regime. He succeeded in having the country's constitution amended to remove the limit on the president serving more than two successive terms. In all likelihood, Xi Jinping will remain in power well beyond 2023, possibly for life. Due to his very personalized style of power compared with his predecessors' relative focus on the Party, his exaltation of Chinese national sentiment and his total control over the Party, Xi is often viewed as the most powerful and authoritarian ruler of communist China since Mao. The "thought" or ideology of Xi Jinping was enshrined in the doctrine and constitution of the Party, a privilege that had previously been reserved for Mao and Deng Xiaoping. Xi Jinping has also cultivated a cult of personality as did Mao Zedong.

Communist China has tirelessly fought against the Western ideals of democracy and individual freedoms — universal values that could corrupt and threaten the Party's hold on society and undermine the foundations of the legitimacy of the CCP. In December 1948, the China of Chiang Kai-shek was one of the founding member countries of the Universal Declaration of Human Rights adopted at the UN. But today communist China does not respect its fundamental principles. This paranoia over Western ideas and values, to which China has been exposed by the policy of openness carried out for forty years, has clearly been accentuated under the reign of Xi Jinping. In November 2019, in the light of massive demonstrations in Hong Kong, the Party's Central Committee issued guidelines to strengthen "patriotic education" in schools, universities and among people from all walks of life. "We must use education to cultivate patriotic feelings in order to train the new generation to produce a new generation which adheres to socialism," the document emphasized. (Gao, 2019)

The ideological takeover has also manifested itself against religions, which have seen a boom in interest in recent years. Since the autumn of 2019, a large sign declaring "10,000 years to the glorious Chinese Communist Party" adorns the facade of Jokhang, the most sacred temple of the Tibetans in Lhasa. Xi Jinping's portraits have replaced those of the Virgin Mary in some churches in China. (Tang, 2019) The Chinese Communist Party has drawn lessons from the collapse of the Soviet Union and the disappearance of the Soviet Communist Party in 1990 and has stood vigilant against subversive Western ideologies. In a speech he delivered to new members and alternates of the Central Committee on January 5, 2013, Xi Jinping emphasized the importance of ideology:

> "Why did the Soviet Union collapse? Why did the Communist Party of the Soviet Union lose power? An important reason is that in the ideological domain the competition was fierce: the historical experience of the Soviet Union was repudiated, the history of the CPSU was repudiated, Lenin was repudiated, Stalin was repudiated, and such historical nihilism did its work... Never deny socialism and Marxism, do not let yourself be influenced by the 'hostile forces' who want to 'westernize' the country and 'sow separatism'. Particular attention should be paid to 'Maneuvers by financial and ideological powers', the use of NGOs, 'their desire to incite chaos by favoring government by the street'": this is a summary of the "Xi Jinping thought". (Bougon, 2017: 47, 50)

In an article published in 2013 entitled "Improving the ideological and political work of young teachers in high schools and universities", Xi Jinping listed the "seven taboos" that must not be discussed in public by officials of the State, including teachers:

> The universal values of human rights and democratic constitutional government; the freedom of the press; civil society; the rights of citizens; past mistakes of the Chinese Communist Party; the financial and political elite; the independence of the judiciary. (Qiao, 2019)

The journalist Gao Yu, born in 1944, was arrested after the massacre in Tiananmen Square in the spring of 1989. Since then, she has been imprisoned several times. In 2014, the authorities accused her of forwarding to a dissident Chinese website based abroad "Document n°9", a text of the CCP Central Committee warning against "the seven perils" that include Western constitutional democracy, the universal values of human rights, civil society, freedom of the press and liberalism. (Bougon, 2019: 143)

Former German Foreign Minister Joschka Fischer believes that:

> Ideologically, the Chinese leadership's rejection of human rights, democracy, and the rule of law is based on the contention that these supposedly universal values are a mere stalking horse for western interests, and that repudiating them should thus be viewed as a matter of self-respect. (Fischer, 2012)

After decades of a benevolent attitude towards China, which was seen as an ally, the tide turned suddenly in Washington at the beginning of the 2010s. The American perception switched to one of China as a threat to the United States and the world, and that view transcended the main political cleavage in American politics to be embraced by both Republicans and Democrats. In 2015, Barack Obama declared in his State of the Union address: "But as we speak, China wants to write the rules for the world's fastest-growing region. That would put our workers and our businesses at a disadvantage. Why would we let that happen? We should write those rules."

John Mearsheimer, an American political scientist who belongs to the realist school of thought on international relations, goes further and argues that the United States should do everything to ensure that China's economy collapses to prevent the emergence of "a new giant Hong Kong" — a greater potential threat than anything America has ever dealt with before. (Keck, 2014) Philip Golub, a professor of international relations at the American University in Paris, explains this turnaround:

> The current administration wants to slow China's ascent by getting rid of the rules, and with Congress and broad sectors of the national security apparatus, has framed China as a major if not yet existential threat: an enormous country that has become too rich too quickly... (Golub, 2019)

Speaking at a symposium at the New America Foundation in Washington in April 2019, when she was director of policy planning at the US State Department, Kiron Skinner said that "China represents a fundamental long-term threat" to the United States that is more serious than that posed by the former Soviet Union. (*ibid.*) In October 2019,

US Secretary of State Mike Pompeo explained, in his view, just how hostile China had become to Western ideas:

> We accommodated and encouraged China's rise for decades, even when — even when that rise was at the expense of American values, Western democracy, and security, and good common sense... The Chinese Communist Party is a Marxist-Leninist Party focused on struggle and international domination. We need only listen to the words of their leaders... Today, we're finally realizing the degree to which the Chinese Communist Party is truly hostile to the United States and our values. (Pompeo, 2019)

The following month, America's top diplomat said the Chinese Communist Party was "shaping a new vision of authoritarianism" and in January 2020 he called it the "central threat of our time". The Sino-American rivalry does not cease to fester and risks becoming a geostrategic confrontation. UN Secretary-General Antonio Guterres has warned of the threat of a profound division developing in the world. "I fear the possibility of a great fracture: the world splitting in two, with the two largest economies on earth creating two separate and competing worlds, each with their own dominant currency, trade and financial rules, their own internet and artificial intelligence capacities, and their own zero-sum geopolitical and military strategies," he declared at the podium of the United Nations General Assembly in September 2019.

Since the historic visit to China by US President Richard Nixon in 1972, which led to the establishment of diplomatic relations on January 1, 1979, relations between China and the United States have gone through ups and downs. For Richard Nixon, in the midst of the Cold War, the United States had found a new ally to counter the influence of the great Soviet enemy, "the Evil Empire" as it was later dubbed by President Ronald Reagan. Although official Chinese ideology categorically rejects US political doctrine, there has nevertheless been a kind of fascination for America among the Chinese. Meanwhile, for the United States, relations with China have now become frankly acrimonious. On both sides a kind of love-hate relationship has developed. But America is probably the only country that an uncompromising China still fears today. So much so that it must, willy-nilly, put up with the fact that the United States delivers weapons to Taiwan to ensure the island's defense against the army of the increasingly threatening mainland. Even though Washington is committed to recognizing only one China of which Taiwan is an integral part, American military assistance to Taiwan in case of an attempted invasion by the People's Liberation Army (PLA) has been enshrined in American law since 1979 by the Taiwan Relations Act. This particular situation profoundly irritates Chinese leaders, who must however resign themselves to it.

The abandonment by the United States of its benevolent policy towards China and the recognition that Beijing has become its main rival led President Donald Trump to unleash a wide range of economic and commercial measures since 2018 when he imposed a number of customs tariffs. He fired a second round at Chinese products in August 2019. From now on, Chinese imports are subject to customs duties varying between 15% and 30%. At the same time, the United States decried large-scale theft of American high-tech secrets and the systematic plunder of intellectual property by China via a vast network of industrial espionage that Trump administration officials said had cost millions of US jobs. Donald Trump never hid his distrust of Chinese economic policy. The US trade deficit with China ($420 billion in 2018 and $353 billion in 2019) undermined his project to "make America great again".

Following the first wave of tariffs, Chinese authorities agreed to negotiate. After fits and starts, the negotiations yielded a preliminary, "phase one" deal that went into effect in early 2020. But there is nothing to say that they will one day reach a "phase two" — Trump said in July 2020 that one wasn't under consideration — let alone a global agreement between the world's two major economies. That is due in no small part to the intense US resentment and desire to slow down the rising power of its rival. We are witnessing a trade war led by the United States, the consequences of which are worrying as it risks aggravating the global recession triggered by the COVID-19 pandemic. But the fact remains that for the first time since the beginning of its economic rise, China has been forced to negotiate. It has, however, stubbornly refused to make any concessions that would see it lose even a smidgen of its national sovereignty. China's desire to become the world's top economy — and even the world's top power — poses a dilemma for US leaders. Either they continue allowing China's economic influence to spread or they attempt, without any certainty of success, to "contain" China. It should be noted that Donald Trump, despite the antics of his capricious foreign policy, often conducted by nocturnal tweets, was the first leader to dare to take the bull by the horns and face the mighty China. This race for world leadership will push the two rivals more and more towards becoming open adversaries. The two countries are competing for control of vast areas of influence around the world and their political systems are becoming increasingly incompatible and antagonistic.

In the United States, inflammatory books have been published to denounce the Chinese peril. One of them, *Death by China: Confronting the Dragon, A Global Call to Action* (Navarro & Autry, 2011), said China "is rapidly turning into the planet's most efficient assassin." Co-author Peter Navarro wrote: "Unscrupulous Chinese entrepreneurs are flooding world markets with lethal products." Navarro, who went on to become Trump's chief trade advisor, also wrote that "China's perverse form of capitalism combines illegal mercantilist and protectionist weapons to pick off American industries, job by job."

Political scientist Graham Allison, a professor at the John F. Kennedy School of Government at Harvard University and former adviser to several secretaries of state and defense, for his part calmly analyzes the current tensions between the two countries that could lead them to the precipice of war. (Allison, 2019 [2017]) He coined the term Thucydides' trap for the dangerous dynamic that is triggered when an ascendant power threatens to overthrow an established power.

As a rapidly ascending China challenges America's accustomed predominance, the two nations risk falling into a deadly trap first identified by the ancient Greek historian Thucydides. Writing about a war that devastated the two leading city-states of classical Greece two and a half millennia ago… It was the rise of Athens and the fear that this instilled in Sparta that made war inevitable. (*ibid.*)

Allison warns that when two countries are engaged in such a rivalry, external events or actions by third parties, which would otherwise be inconsequential or easy to manage, may trigger actions and reactions from the main protagonists that result in a war that neither of them wanted.

War between the United States and China is not inevitable, but it is possible. Indeed, as these scenarios illustrate the underlying stress created by China's disruptive rise creates conditions in which accidental, otherwise inconsequential events could trigger a large-scale conflict. (*ibid.*)

Former US Secretary of State Henry Kissinger, the architect of Sino-American rapprochement fifty years ago, warned in November 2019 that unless China and the United States resolve their differences, a conflict would be "inevitable" and result in "a catastrophic outcome" that "will be worse than world wars". (Browne, 2019) Speaking at the same conference, Chinese Vice-President Wang Qishan highlighted the need to restore better relations between his country and the United States. "Between war and peace, the Chinese people firmly choose peace. Humanity cherishes peace. We should abandon the zero-sum thinking and cold war mentality." (Martin, Han, Li *et al.*, 2019)

In their book *La Chine contre l'Amérique, le duel du siècle (China vs. America: The Duel of the Century)*, the *Le Monde* journalists Alain Frachon and Daniel Vernet (2012) argued that the US and Chinese economies are becoming increasingly interdependent and the two countries "have an interest in the other prospering" but that a "clash is inevitable" between Beijing and Washington. "Everything contributes, history, the balance of forces, special interests and the interests of third countries, the fantasies entertained on both sides," the two authors emphasized. "The epicenter of the next earthquake is in the Pacific," they concluded. It should be noted that Chinese ultra-nationalists no longer hesitate to proclaim that China must become number one in the world and thus take the upper hand over the United States. Among those in this influential political fringe in Beijing, there is the famous PLA Colonel Liu Mingfu, an ex-professor at the National Defense University and author of an incendiary 2010 book *The China Dream*.

"The Chinese people must understand that between us and the United States there is only one issue: Who will be number one? Our dream is to become number one. To become the greatest world power. This will be our way of participating in a world without a hegemonic power because China, you see, cannot exercise its power in a dominant way like the United States does… In the world, there must always be a champion, a power stronger than others, but we will embody a new style of champion, a non-hegemonic champion. This is why the world will be better when China is number one," explains Colonel Liu Mingfu. (Frachon & Vernet, 2012)

The notion of the "China dream" was taken up in 2012 by President Xi Jinping, and it remains a current slogan, regularly put forward by the government in Beijing. The "China dream" is a mixture of economic reform and vehement nationalism. According to political scientist Xiang Lanxin, the formula reflects three objectives: "To restore the past glory of China and the state, to emphasize the secular desire for a modern China that is as rich and powerful as what the emperors had, and finally to make the Chinese proud and happy, in order to maintain social stability." Sinologist Michel Jan[3] believes the "Chinese dream" is "just a new stage in the political life of the regime after the campaigns and slogans that have marked the history of the PRC since 1949." (Jan, 2013)

After the "peaceful rise in power" and "the peaceful development", here is "the China dream" and the "Great renaissance of the Chinese people". We can expect that this slogan will mark the entire decade of the Xi Jinping era, with successive adaptations, until 2022 (the year of the 20th Congress of the CCP), and see the outcome in 2049 (the 100th anniversary of the PRC). (Jan, 2013)

For Jan, this new political slogan has a strong nationalist connotation. Bertrand Badie, a professor of international relations at the Paris Institute of Political Studies (Sciences–Po), believes no one will win this Chinese-American duel. "We have, since 20 years ago, changed the

---

[3] Michel Jan, a career soldier and China expert who is the author of numerous books, specializes in international relations and the Far East, with a particular interest in the market regions of the Chinese Empire.

software. We no longer win wars. We are in a situation, in the current confrontation, where everyone loses. We are in a new world that has changed software" where the great powers are interdependent, he said in an appearance on *The Debate* program on France's Arte channel in August 2019. He said the danger is that "we go from a trade confrontation to a multisectoral confrontation" as China pursues its effort to become a regional power in Asia and the United States steps up its military posture, as with the August 2019 announcement of the deployment of new missiles in the Asian theater to protect its allies. It is a similar view to that of Graham Allison, where conflict is the result of rivalry gone awry, of misunderstandings and miscalculations made. Moreover, traditional Chinese military strategic thinking also favors avoiding hostilities if possible. "Victory is not the simple triumph of the armed forces", but "the achievement of the ultimate political objectives that the military conflict was supposed to ensure" stated the 5th century BC Chinese general Sun Tzu. "The supreme art of war is to subdue the enemy without fighting" and "instead of provoking the enemy on the battlefield, better to skillfully lead him to an unfavorable position where it will be impossible to extricate himself," he added.

Meanwhile, the European Union for the first time outlined a unified policy towards China at a summit in Brussels in April 2019. In a seven-page joint statement, Brussels and Beijing agreed to fight "protectionism" and work towards "strengthening international rules on industrial subsidies" as part of a reform of the World Trade Organization. While the EU now recognizes China as a systemic rival, Prime Minister Li Keqiang has pledged to promote trade "based on rules" and "to facilitate access of European companies" to his country's market, even if today they are often victims of discrimination, opaque regulations, restrictions on their investments or forced technology transfers. The EU is in theory the most important economic partner of China, which is the second EU trade partner after the United States. Most of this trade involves industrial and manufactured goods. Still, China and the United States have both discreetly rejoiced at European divisions in general, and the January 31, 2020 exit of the United Kingdom from the EU in particular.

Since forging diplomatic relations with the EU in 1975, Chinese economic strategy towards the European Union has changed. Ostensibly abandoning Brussels, China has chosen to cultivate bilateral relations with individual EU countries — mainly with Germany, now its privileged interlocutor. This change in strategy, as Institute of International Relations and Strategic Affairs (IRIS) analyst Olivia Meudec noted, "is explained by China's awareness of the EU's weaknesses — both organic and political — which it chooses to exploit to its advantage."

> Indeed, the Chinese strategy has not changed without reason: faced with a disunited European Union incapable of proposing a coherent political line vis-à-vis Beijing, the PRC preferred to abandon Brussels institutions which have shown their structural weaknesses. Bilateral relations between each EU member and China flourish and deepen in equal measure as the Sino–European relationship, that is with the EU in its entirety, fades. (Meudec, 2017)

For political scientist Caroline Galactéros, a councilor at France's Institute of Higher Studies of National Defense, the European Union must build greater political unity to be able to face the China/US duopoly. The blow of the bloc's abandonment by the US may give a welcome impetus to this process.

> It is our utopias that are in disarray and it's good that Europe is falling into strategic insignificance (a form of brain death) after having suddenly been deprived of the mental crutch provided by the transatlantic link and its servile alignment with American injunctions… Our old continent is in the midst of untreated post-traumatic depression. The shock? Our abandonment without hesitation by the American father figure… Beijing acts in exactly the same manner as Washington and plays European countries off against one another… China is benefiting from this tension between Washington and the Europeans as European countries realize that they can no longer count upon America. (Galactéros, 2019)

French President Emmanuel Macron outlined what the EU's relations with China should be in an August 2019 speech to ambassadors. He said the world order is being disrupted in an unprecedented way with the crisis in the market economy, the end of Western hegemony and the emergence of new powers, pointing to "China first and foremost". Macron said ways to shape globalization as well as reshape this international order must be found or "Europe will disappear... and the world will be centered around two main focal points: the United States and China." Given that China doesn't share the same values as Europe, Macron said Europe needs to help "build a new order in which not only would we have a role to play, but so would our values and interests..." The French president said this would "restore what is essentially European civilization" enthused with the spirit of the Renaissance and the Enlightenment. He said it was a "humanist project" that reinvests in human beings through educational, social and healthcare projects while pursuing a crucial ecological transformation. Macron also called for the European Union to "revisit" the Pacific region to "regain the respect of China". (Macron, 2019)

The Sino-American crisis has been aggravated further by the novel coronavirus pandemic, with the world's top two powers regularly trading insults. These exchanges include US Attorney General William Barr accusing China in July 2020 of wanting to replace the United States as the world's top economic and military power with the help of US institutions. "The People's Republic of China is now engaged in an economic blitzkrieg — an aggressive, orchestrated, whole-of-government (indeed, whole-of-society) campaign to seize the commanding heights of the global economy and to surpass the United States as the world's preeminent superpower," Barr said in a speech at the Gerald R. Ford Presidential Museum in Michigan. "The CCP rules with an iron fist over one of the great ancient civilizations of the world. It seeks to leverage the immense power, productivity, and ingenuity of the Chinese people to overthrow the rules-based international system and to make the world safe for dictatorship," said the Attorney General. "As all of these examples should make clear, the ultimate ambition of China's rulers isn't to trade with the United States. It is to raid the United States," he said. For American businesses "appeasing the PRC may bring short-term rewards. But in the end, the PRC's goal is to replace you." Two days later, Chinese Foreign Minister Wang Yi told his

Russian counterpart Sergey Lavrov that the United States "has used the epidemic to smear other countries and shift the blame in every possible way, and even created hot spots and confrontation in international relations. It has lost its sense of reason, morality and credibility." Wang added during the phone call with Lavrov that the "United States is practicing its policy of stark 'America First' and pursuing its egoism, unilateralism and bullying policy to the extreme. It has failed to fulfill its responsibilities commensurate with its status." Donald Trump launched a salvo on June 30, pinning the blame on China for the propagation of the novel coronavirus around the world. "As I watch the Pandemic spread its ugly face all across the world, including the tremendous damage it has done to the USA, I become more and more angry at China," Trump tweeted.

While we are rapidly becoming inured to the idea of China and the US being in confrontation, we should keep in perspective just how new this is, according to John Delury, a professor of Chinese studies at Yonsei University Graduate School of International Studies in Seoul.

> For the first time in centuries, Americans are looking upon China as an equal in terms of national wealth and power; and this parity presents itself as a threat to the interests and security of the United States. By putting this perception of China as a *rival* in historical context, we can appreciate just how novel and uncharted the territory ahead for the two nations is.

On July 22, 2020, Sino-American tensions were ratcheted higher when the US State Department announced that the Chinese consulate in Houston, Texas must close within 72 hours, an unprecedented move in the history of US-Chinese diplomatic relations. "The United States will not tolerate the PRC's violations of our sovereignty and intimidation of our people, just as we have not tolerated the PRC's unfair trade practices, theft of American jobs, and other egregious behavior," State Department spokeswoman Morgan Ortagus said in announcing the closure. "The Vienna Convention states diplomats must 'respect the laws and regulations of the receiving state' and 'have a duty not to interfere in the internal affairs of that state,'" she added. Meanwhile, US Secretary of State Mike Pompeo said the Chinese consulate in

Houston had become "a hub of spying and intellectual property theft." He added that "China ripped off our prized intellectual property and trade secrets, costing millions of jobs all across America." China's response did not take long in coming. Two days later it ordered the closure of the US consulate in the city of Chengdu. The closure of the consulate in the southwestern Sichuan region is not without consequences as it was responsible for monitoring all of southwestern China, including the autonomous region of Tibet. According to its internet site, it had 200 staff, 150 of whom were local employees. Pompeo delivered on July 23 a diatribe against China that recalled Cold War-era language about the Soviet Union. "The free world must triumph over this new tyranny," he said in a speech entitled "Communist China and the free world's future". "… today China is increasingly authoritarian at home and more aggressive in its hostility to freedom everywhere else," added Pompeo. The same month he called for like-minded nations to build a "coalition" against China. "We want every nation to work together to push back against the Chinese Communist Party's efforts in every dimension that I have described," he said during a visit to London.

Chapter 2

The Rivalry Between
Two Economic Models

The United States, the world's leading economic power, is the champion of the economic liberalism that has long been held up as an example to the world. This hegemonic model is today colliding with a new form of directed capitalism wielded by communist China which has enjoyed an unparalleled spurt of development over the past four decades. China now holds up its model triumphantly, although it has recorded its first economic setbacks. What we have today is a tale of growing rivalry. Faced with US sanctions, China has been forced to negotiate for the first time in forty years. The first steps down the path towards economic and political war have thus been taken and the consequences of this remain unknown.

"As soon as there is rivalry, even hidden, influence fades away; the other must be removed, even overwritten."

Francoise Giroud

Si je mens (If I Lie)

Paris Stock, 1972

China was an impoverished country mired in underdevelopment in the 1970s at the start of its economic reforms. It accounted for only 3.1% of global gross domestic product (GDP) in 1970. Since 1979, China has experienced extraordinary economic development, any description of which is forcibly littered with superlatives. China's GDP has grown more than tenfold in the last fifteen years, while during the same period that of the United States has only doubled. In 1960, America's supremacy was overwhelming, with a GDP of $543 billion compared to China's $60 billion. In 2018, the United States was still largely in the lead with a GDP of $21.34 trillion, against $14.2 trillion for China, according to figures from the International Monetary Fund (IMF). But in terms of purchasing power parity (PPP), China is now ranked first with a GDP per capita of $18,210. From 2000 to 2010, China accounted for 33% of global growth in absolute terms. China has since 2010 been the world's top exporter, top industrial power and the second-largest importer, just behind the European Union. Its foreign exchange reserves reached some $3.15 trillion in October 2019. China is by far the biggest holder of US treasury bonds, with a total of $1.27 trillion in 2019.

China has also become the largest official lender of capital in the world, going from nearly zero loans granted in 2000 to more than $700 billion accorded in 2019, double the figure for the IMF and the World Bank combined. (A new study, 2019) A major difference is that the IMF grants its loans in total transparency, while Chinese loans are often 'hidden' — never reported — and accorded to vulnerable borrowers such as Iran, Venezuela and Zimbabwe. (*ibid.*) China's development of its export industry, coupled with wage moderation that slowed down consumption, has generated a gigantic current account surplus which peaked at almost 10% of GDP in 2017. The current account corresponds to a country's goods trade balance (exports–imports), to which trade in services and income transfers (repatriation of profits, sending of money by immigrant workers) are added. And by running a surplus, a country is in effect lending to the world.

China's growth rate consistently exceeded 10% in the 1980s and 1990s. It has slowed considerably since 2010, to 6.8% in 2017, 6.6% in 2018 and 6.1% in 2019, which was the lowest growth rate for 29 years, but which was nevertheless double the world average. This deceleration, while still moderate, is noticeable and has been the cause of more than a little worry for Chinese leaders, who know that strong growth is a necessary condition for calm and stability on the social front. According to IMF economists, China has entered a phase of "structural slowdown". US trade sanctions have begun to weigh on Chinese GDP. Some economists believe that the slowdown in growth reflects the consequence of a progressive and welcome evolution of the Chinese economy rather than a deep derailment that could portend a serious crisis. In this view, the Chinese economy has matured from the period of rapid industrialization, and like other industrialized nations growth will now be slower and be driven more by domestic consumption and gains in efficiency. Others are less optimistic and believe that China will not be able to sustain growth, due mainly to lackluster domestic consumption, the threat of a major financial crisis with a public debt that continues to climb, and government policies that have limited the expansion of the private sector. Growth could drop below 4% from 2030. At the beginning of September 2020, Xi Jinping warned that China must retool its economy to be more self-sustaining in a post-pandemic world of uncertainty, weakened demand and hostility. China needs its people to spend more and its manufacturers to be more innovative, Xi said, to ease its dependence on fickle foreign economies. But nevertheless, over the past forty years China has racked up a long list of successes. Between 1978 and 2013, very rapid economic growth made it possible to increase average adult income severalfold. This resulted in 800 million Chinese rising above the poverty line. China similarly reduced its infant mortality rate by 85%. The Chinese economy, which represented 10% of the US economy in 2007, is expected to outweigh it by more than 50% in 2023 and, according to IMF forecasts, it could be three times larger in 2040.

This extraordinary economic development relied in great part upon the benevolent attitude of the United States towards China and a very significant strengthening of their economic and commercial cooperation. In 2001, after long negotiations that lasted over fifteen years, China officially became a member of the World Trade Organization (WTO). This major diplomatic breakthrough for Beijing was assisted by the United States. In fact, the relationship between the United States and China enjoyed a considerable boom throughout the 1980s and 1990s. The opening engineered by Beijing aimed to learn and copy as much as possible from foreign experience, in particular that of the United States. Understanding the American economy and society was a priority. Deng Xiaoping made a trip to the United States in 1979 where he didn't hesitate to put on a cowboy hat. The historic visit, broadcast on Chinese television, caused a sensation — a real psychological shock. Later high-ranking PLA officers visited the US Army's training academy, West Point. Above all, "many Chinese students were allowed to study in American universities," according to Richard Arzt, a journalist specializing in China. (Arzt, 2019) Some 363,000 Chinese were studying in the United States in 2018, including 36% in science and technology fields, engineering and mathematics, according to the Institute of International Education (IIE), an American organization based in New York. Xi Mingze, Xi Jinping's only daughter, studied at Harvard University and graduated in 2014. "On the American side, interest in China turned to infatuation," says Claude Martin, who served as France's ambassador to China in 1990–1993 and is the author of the book *La diplomatie n'est pas un dîner de gala* (*Diplomacy is Not a Gala Dinner*). (Martin, 2018) In the early 1980s, when serving as the number two diplomat in the French Embassy in Beijing, he recalled that:

> In all areas, the United States considered the Chinese as partners: to be taken care of, helped, provided with all the necessary assistance. The illusion was to believe that China was becoming a democracy. However, it was only walking down the path of reforms. (Martin, 2018)

Since 1979, China has adopted a new economic system, which it presents as a "socialist market economy", that has replaced the planned economy. In this new model, economic liberalism and authoritarian political control rub shoulders in a marriage that has proven its dynamism for forty years. The state owns the means of production, and a centralized authority determines the prices. The private sector is encouraged and plays a growing role in the economy. The public sector's share thus shrank from 73% of industrial production in 1988 to only 35% in 1992. Meanwhile, the private sector now represents 60% of the country's GDP and 80% of urban employment.

This transformation of the Chinese economy has at the same time created very significant social disparities. The gap between the newly rich and the poor has not stopped widening. In 2016, China's Gini coefficient, one of the most commonly used measures of inequality in the distribution of income, came in at 0.461 on a scale of 0 to 1. The most egalitarian countries such as Denmark, Sweden and Japan, have scores of around 0.2. Meanwhile, the most unequal countries such as Brazil, Guatemala and Honduras, have scores around 0.6. Curiously enough, China was more egalitarian than the United States that year, as the US Census Bureau calculated its Gini coefficient at 0.481, although researchers at the Pew Research Center note that when all taxes and transfers are taken into account the US scores better than China. (Horowitz, Igielnik and Kochhar, 2020)

If China's Gini coefficient has been in decline since 2008, the year when the country recorded a peak at 0.49, it remains at a high level and is a sign of persistent social inequalities. The income gap between the cities and the countryside is considerable and the magnitude of these inequalities is a source of discontent among the population and a point of concern for the regime. The average annual net income of rural inhabitants was 12,363 yuan (around 1,682 euros or $1,860 at average 2016 exchange rates) in 2016, while in urban areas it was 33,616 yuan per person (almost 4,573 euros or $5,055). The inequalities between China's rural and urban areas are not limited to income. Urban people have better access to social housing and a more extensive social welfare system, in particular retirement benefits. China's poor and most vulnerable people are found above all among farmers and retirees in rural areas as well as migrant workers (*mingong*) who flee the countryside to look for a job in the big eastern and southeastern cities. Their rural residence permits mean they cannot access public services and benefits in the cities where they have found work.

Another consequence of this new economic equilibrium is the appearance of a new middle class that is growing steadily. The upper-middle class should account for a third of the Chinese population within 15 years, or 480 million inhabitants. It is a revolution to come in terms of consumption. In 2030, the purchasing power of the

Chinese will be similar to that of South Korea today and that of the United States in 2000, according to a 2016 paper by *The Economist Intelligence Unit*.[1] "By 2030 China will look and feel like a more middle-class society, although wealth inequalities will represent an important social challenge," it said. It is this middle class that fed an increasingly important flow of Chinese tourists around the world before the COVID-19 pandemic. They accounted for only 11% of international tourists in 2018, but according to UN World Tourism Organization data, accounted for a fifth of total spending. Even if the number of Chinese traveling abroad was growing rapidly, jumping by 15% in 2018, there is plenty of room for growth as only 10% of Chinese have a passport. While tourism figures collapsed in 2020 as a result of the COVID-19 pandemic, Chinese tourists are likely to play an important role in the eventual recovery of the sector.

China's blockbuster growth has also created a rising number of millionaires. Over the coming years, China should see its number of millionaires jump by 62% to reach 5.65 million in 2023. With an additional 2.12 million millionaires compared to 2018, it is on the way to becoming the world's number two country in terms of the number of people with more than $1 million in wealth, behind the United States. When it comes to dollar billionaires, it already passed its rival in 2015. There were 62 Chinese fortunes over $2 billion in 2019, of which 32 were more than $10 billion. (HRI, 2019a) It is a result corroborated by the annual barometer of Crédit Suisse, which has identified 100 million Chinese among the richest 10% in the world in 2019, compared to 99 million Americans. According to the study, the total wealth of Chinese households increased 17-fold in less than 20 years, going from $3,697 in 2000 to $63,762 in 2019. While there are still many more millionaires in the United States (18 million) than in China (4.4 million), the gap is narrowing. Despite the Sino-American trade war, these two countries were the two main contributors to the 2.6% increase of global wealth from mid-2018 to mid-2019. This study shows, however, that inequalities are widening in China since 1% of

---

[1] http://country.eiu.com/article.aspx?articleid=1584774142.

the Chinese owned 30% of the wealth of the country. (Crédit Suisse, 2019) It is true that inequalities are deepening all over the world. According to the annual report of the British NGO Oxfam, 2,153 billionaires around the world have more money than the 4.6 billion poorest people. (*Time to Care*, 2020)

Against this new Chinese economic model stands the United States with its model of economic liberalism. "The inhabitant of the United States learns from birth that one must rely upon oneself to fight against the inconveniences in life; he casts a defiant and worried look upon social authority, and only appeals to its power when one cannot do without it." This is how Alexis de Tocqueville, having returned from the United States in 1840, summarized the values of the American system. That everyone has the potential to succeed by relying only on his innate qualities. That everyone must strive to further push back the "frontier" (whether it be geographic or social). That private enterprise, the principle of competition and the market economy are the engines of activity for the country. (de Tocqueville 2019 [1835]) It is true that the industrial boom of the nineteenth century transformed the country. Already technological innovations and the use of machine tools in the United States exceeded that in Europe. Alexander Graham Bell invented the telephone in 1875. In 1900, the United States counted one million installed telephones. Between 1860 and 1890, industrial production multiplied by 11! The United States became the world's largest producer of coal. In 1873, income per capita overtook that of the United Kingdom, which had hitherto been the world's leading economic power. America went on to achieve further economic successes. At the beginning of the twentieth century, it occupied first place on the podium of economic powers of the planet, a rank it did not cede until now. The 1929 New York stock market crash marked the start of the Great Depression, the greatest economic crisis of the twentieth century. But the United States recovered from it and remained the world champion.

Under Donald Trump's presidency, the country's economic performance remained positive until the COVID-19 pandemic struck in 2020. GDP growth reached 2.9% in 2018 and 2.3% in 2019. In fact, the vast territory of the United States is full of natural resources and exports an impressive amount of physical and cultural goods. The country remains the number one recipient of foreign direct investment. The US dollar serves as the world's reserve currency. Money is a tool of sovereignty and reflects the weight and economic power of a country. At the end of World War II, the United held three-quarters of the world's gold reserves, according to Malika Smaïli. (Laprée, Smaïli, Grosdet *et al.*, 2018) The Bretton Woods Agreement, signed in July 1944, "laid the foundations of the international financial system and confirmed the hegemony of the American economy, making the dollar the linchpin of the new world monetary organization: the dollar was thus established as the reserve currency," she wrote. (*ibid.*)

The dollar being a global reserve currency confers an advantage onto the United States. As the greenback is the de facto global currency for trade, other nations have to hold a certain amount of it. In fact, they are usually willing to hold more, and not in cash but in debt. This is the essence of what happens when they run a trade surplus with the United States — they are selling goods in exchange for US debt. As this debt is in dollars, the US runs no currency exchange risk and can generally find more takers of its debt. But this means the United States can go deeper into debt. From 2008 to 2016, public debt almost doubled from $10 trillion to $19 trillion. Foreign investors and countries acquire much of that debt — in 2019 they held over a quarter of US government debt with China at the top. One can thus say the United States has had its economic development partially financed by the world community. Another, less generous, interpretation is that the economic partners of the United States have underwritten the standard of living of Americans. The sudden drop in economic activity due to COVID-19 lockdowns and added expenses for relief measures are expected to drive the US budget deficit much higher. The Committee for a Responsible Federal Budget, a non-profit advocacy group, estimated in September that it will quadruple to $3.8 trillion, or 18.7% of GDP.

China has not stood still in the face of this monetary hegemony. Since 2010, it has started to use the yuan or renminbi (RMB) as the reference currency with some of its trading partners. First in Southeast

Asia, then with other countries around the world. In 2014, the Chinese currency, although it cannot be freely bought and sold, supplanted Australian and Canadian dollars to rank as the fifth largest payment currency in the world. One year later, the IMF accepted the inclusion of the yuan in its currency basket used for Special Drawing Rights (SDRs). Since then, the yuan has continued to make inroads internationally. In 2017, the central banks of more than 60 countries and regions kept reserves of yuan, according to the People's Bank of China (PBOC). But the influence of the dollar is not weakening. According to IMF data from 2018, the greenback represented 64% of central bank assets, a ratio that is out of proportion to the size of the American economy, which accounts for only 20% of global GDP. The euro holds the second position (20%), very far ahead of the Japanese yen and the pound sterling (4.5% each). At 1.12%, the yuan is still almost nonexistent, although China can be proud of doing better than the Swiss franc (0.17%)! Donald Trump and his administration regularly accused China of using its currency as a commercial weapon by maintaining the yuan at an artificially low level against the dollar. Although Beijing rejects these accusations, the Chinese currency has in recent years seen a gentle erosion of its value. Then, on August 5, 2019, at the height of the Sino-American trade war, the Chinese central bank ostensibly withdrew support for the yuan, which suddenly tumbled below the 7 yuan per dollar threshold to its lowest level since 2008, thus making Chinese exports more competitive. Donald Trump immediately accused China of "manipulating its currency". The accusation was flatly rejected by Beijing, which called on Washington "to rein in its horse before falling over the cliff, recognize its mistake by turning back from the wrong path." Overall, despite China's efforts to promote the yuan on the international stage, the US dollar remains the only global reserve currency.

Meanwhile, China has become the world champion in patent applications, an indicator of a country's industrial innovation. Filing of patent applications and registration of trademarks, designs and industrial models around the world reached record levels in 2019, driven by the surge in China, where nearly half of the world's patent applications were filed. These overall figures need to be considered with caution, however. The vast majority of the patent applications were only filed in China and only a fraction was for breakthrough inventions, with most only providing minimal modifications to existing patents. But in 2019 China for the first time surpassed the United States in international patent applications, according to the World Intellectual Property Organization (WIPO). There were 58,990 Chinese requests submitted via WIPO's patent cooperation treaty system compared with 57,840 from the United States.

Trade between the United States and China has long been lopsided in China's favor. The US trade deficit with China reached $419.2 billion in 2018 (out of a total of approximately $600 billion), a 10-year high, and then decreased slightly in 2019. In order to correct this, Washington has called on Beijing to implement structural reforms that would prohibit government subsidies to public enterprises, ban forced technology transfers by foreign companies that set up shop in China, and purchase more American products, especially agricultural goods. China had long turned a deaf ear to such calls, so US President Donald Trump decided in January 2018 to take action, slapping customs duties on washing machines and solar panels, which de facto targeted China. In retaliation, China launched an anti-dumping investigation into American sorghum in February. Then in March Trump signed an order imposing 25% customs duties on imports of aluminum and 10% duties on imported steel, which once again de facto targeted China. In April, he introduced a tariff hike on around 1,300 products from China accounting for $60 billion of imports, including flat screens, weapons, satellites, medical equipment, auto parts and batteries. China responded by announcing a list of 128 products on which customs duties increased by 15%, such as wine and fruits, and eight products on which the increase is 25%, including pork. On April 4, China adopted another list of $50 billion in products, including in particular soybeans, beef, cotton, tobacco, whiskey, and the automotive and aeronautic sectors. The two countries continued to slap tit-for-tat tariff increases upon one another. In July 2018, Trump said he was ready to introduce customs duties on up to $500 billion of Chinese goods, i.e. all Chinese products imported by the United States. As trade tensions mounted the Chinese currency tumbled, which made Chinese exports cheaper in dollar terms, partially negating the effect of the tariffs.

Huawei has found itself at the heart of the confrontation between China and the United States over technology. In August 2018, Trump signed into law a measure that prohibited the US government or any firm that wants to do business with the US government from using equipment from the Chinese telecommunications giant[2], the world's number one manufacturer of smartphones, citing threats to "national security". Huawei Technologies Co was also excluded from supplying equipment for the core of mobile telecommunications networks and since May 2019 has been prohibited from buying electronic components from US manufacturers.[3] Huawei founder Ren Zhengfei, a former Chinese military engineer, has repeatedly denied accusations that the firm carries out espionage on behalf of the PLA or the Chinese government via backdoors that allow access to confidential information.

Washington has asked its allies, with relative success, not to use the Chinese firm for their fifth generation or 5G mobile networks, invoking supposed links between Huawei and Chinese intelligence services. 5G mobile networks, which are 20–100 times faster than today's 4G networks, are expected to enable remotely-directed medical operations, fully autonomous driving, and other data-hungry applications and thus become very sensitive and critical infrastructure. Australia, Britain, Canada, France, India, Israel, New Zealand, and several Eastern European nations have banned purchases of Huawei equipment for their 5G networks, and where the company's tech has already been

---

[2] Huawei is the world's number one smartphone maker, having overtaken Apple in 2019 and Samsung in 2020. The firm, which employs 188,000 people, posted sales of $91.3 billion in 2018. It holds 28% of the global market for telecommunications network equipment, ahead of 17% for Nokia and 13% for Ericsson.

[3] As a result of US sanctions, in September 2019 Huawei was forced to present its new P30 smartphone without the Android operating system and all Google applications, a serious setback for its sales on world markets.

installed, it will be gradually retired. Germany appeared to be moving towards banning Huawei equipment in late 2020.

The banishment of Huawei by a good number of Western countries is a major blow. Even more so since Washington has banned US semiconductor manufacturers (or those using their licenses) from supplying Huawei. The company has acknowledged that the ban puts its future in question. "We are in a difficult situation … Huawei's smartphones have no chip supply," said Richard Yu Chengdong, chief executive of the company's consumer business group. "This year may be the last generation of Huawei Kirin high-end chips … This is a big loss for us," he was quoted as saying by the *South China Morning Post* at an August 2020 presentation.

It must have been a difficult admission for a company that, in a few short years, had managed to surpass South Korea's Samsung as the world's top manufacturer of smartphones. And it wasn't just low-cost models — it had developed its own line of Kirin chips that help power its high-end phones. But as these relied on US technology for their manufacture, Huawei found itself cut off from a key component when Washington tightened restrictions. The development is serious as handsets account for most of Huawei's revenue, which hit $64.2 billion in the first half of 2020. "Huawei looks like it will lose a lot in smartphone sales [without Kirin chips]," Greg Austin, senior fellow for Cyber, Space and Future Conflict at the International Institute for Strategic Studies in Singapore, was quoted as saying by the *South China Morning Post*. The Kirin 900 chip was installed in 36% of Huawei's smartphones shipped in the first quarter of 2020, in both high-end and mid-market models. Richard Yu Chengdong acknowledged that the high-end Mate 40 would probably be the last equipped with the chip.

Huawei will not be the only one getting hurt. In 2018, China imported $310 billion in semiconductors, or 61% of the total manufactured in the world. Manufacturers in the United States, Europe, Japan, South Korea and Taiwan (especially Taiwan Semiconductor Manufacturing Co, or TSMC, which made the Kirin chips) will also suffer from the US sanctions.

But by shifting the front of the Sino-American trade war to semi-conductors, Washington has moved to favorable terrain as Chinese companies are not capable of producing high-performance chips needed for the latest generation of equipment. It will likely take China years to catch up to today's manufacturing technology which engraves circuits that are seven or even just five nanometers wide. Chinese manufacturers can produce chips with circuits of 25 nanometers, a massive difference that puts China at a huge disadvantage in producing a wide range of equipment.

The noose is tightening around Huawei. In August 2020, Secretary of State Mike Pompeo said the "Trump Administration sees Huawei for what it is — an arm of the Chinese Communist Party's surveillance state" as the US government added 38 Huawei subsidiaries to the list of companies banned from receiving sensitive technologies. Meanwhile, Huawei had scrambled to build up a stock of semiconductors that could allow it to hold on for at least several months. Both it and Beijing were evidently hoping for the election of Democrat Joe Biden as president in November 2020 and a shift in US policy towards China.

The dispute has also hit close to home for Huawei's founder Ren Zhengfei. In December 2018, his daughter Meng Wanzhou was detained in the Canadian city of Vancouver at the request of Washington on allegations she violated US sanctions on Iran. Meng, who serves as Huawei's financial director, was placed under house arrest pending extradition to the United States. Soon afterward, Canadians Michael Spavor and Michael Kovrig were arrested in China and placed in detention on suspicions of espionage. In July 2019, a third Canadian national was arrested in China and thrown in jail.[4]

An initial consequence of the Sino-American trade war was that China fell from the rank of America's top trade partner to third place during the January-June 2019 period, behind Mexico and Canada, both in terms of imports and exports. In June 2019, Donald Trump

---

[4] For further reading on the campaign led by Huawei to penetrate European markets, in particular that of France, and on the challenges of 5G, check out Antoine Izambard's *France-Chine. Les liaisons dangereuses* (2019).

and his Chinese counterpart Xi Jinping declared a truce in the trade war. Meeting with Xi on the sidelines of the G20 summit in Osaka, Japan, the US president announced the resumption of trade negotiations that had been suspended for months. The talks quickly resumed, but then on August 1, to everyone's surprise, Trump wrote on his Twitter account that he would impose customs duties of 10% on $300 billion worth of non-taxed Chinese imports beginning the following month. On August 13, he partially backtracked, postponing until December 15 the measure for about fifteen products such as laptops, smartphones, gaming consoles and items related to health and safety. On August 23, China responded by announcing tariffs of between 5 and 10% on $75 billion worth of American products. A few hours later, Donald Trump retaliated blow-for-blow by announcing that from October 1 he would increase the punitive duties on $250 billion worth of goods imported from China from 25 to 30%. In addition, he announced that the 10% duty on $300 billion worth of imports set to go into force on September 1st would in fact be 15%. On August 25, he ordered American companies to withdraw from China, saying they should return home the next day. "We don't need China and, frankly, would be far better off without them," Trump tweeted. "Our economy, because of our gains in the last 2 1/2 years, is MUCH larger than that of China. We will keep it that way!" he added. Just days later on August 26, the US president took a more accommodating approach at the G7 summit in Biarritz, stating that: "China called last night… said let's get back to the table. So we'll be getting back to the table." Trump also estimated the chances of reaching an agreement as better than ever: "I think we're going to make a deal."

The trade dispute between Beijing and Washington has cost companies from both countries billions of dollars. It has disrupted the manufacturing sector and supply chains and, at the same time, caused significant turbulence in global financial markets and risked causing a general economic slowdown even before the COVID-19 pandemic struck. But in his speech to the United Nations General Assembly in September 2019, Trump was still combative. "For years, these abuses [of international trade rules] were tolerated, ignored, or even encouraged…

But as far as America is concerned, those days are over," he said. While China had agreed to negotiate with the United States, it had also warned that it would not bow to American pressure. In May 2019, the *Global Times*, an English-language daily under the control of the Chinese Communist Party mouthpiece the *People's Daily*, wrote:

> China is ready for a long-term trade battle with the US. Compared to last year when the US started the trade war, the Chinese public is more supportive of the government taking tough countermeasures. More and more Chinese people now believe that the real purpose of some Washington elites is to ruin China's development capabilities, and these people have hijacked the US' China policy. (Golub, 2019)

In October 2019, the US Department of Commerce placed 20 Chinese organizations and public companies linked to state security services as well as eight private companies on a blacklist to punish them for repression of the Uighur community in Xinjiang (former East Turkestan). Among these companies, now banned from buying components from American companies without US government approval, figure the video surveillance giant Hikvision and the companies specializing in facial recognition technologies, SenseTime Group and Megvii Technology Ltd.[5] Commerce Secretary Wilbur Ross said the United States "cannot and will not tolerate the brutal suppression of ethnic minorities within China." (Shepardson & Horwitz, 2019) The next day, the US State Department announced a visa ban for all Chinese officials associated with the Chinese repression of the Uighurs in Xinjiang. The Sino-American conflict thus leaped beyond commercial issues. The US has gone from accusations of large-scale systematic

---

[5] Hikvision, valued at $42 billion, is the world's largest manufacturer of video surveillance equipment. SenseTime, valued at $4.5 billion, is one of the most successful unicorns (start-ups valued at over a billion dollars) in the field of artificial intelligence. Other companies targeted by the US sanctions are iFlytec Co which specializes in voice recognition, surveillance equipment manufacturer Dahua Technology, data recovery firm Meiya Pico Information Co, facial recognition company Yitu Technology and Yixin Science and Technology Co.

pillage of American technologies, the theft of know-how in the field of artificial intelligence and unfair trade practices, to an even more serious disillusionment about its relations with China. Washington now criticizes Beijing for rights violations and believes that China harbors territorial ambitions that threaten Asia.

America is now engaged in a long struggle. On October 11, 2019, after two days of negotiations (the Chinese government used the term "consultations") in Washington, the United States and China reached a partial agreement in principle, a "Phase 1" of an intended comprehensive agreement. Under this, America agreed to freeze its planned increase in customs tariffs from 25% to 30% on $250 billion of Chinese imports in exchange for Beijing's promise to buy $50 billion worth of American agricultural products, the introduction of a stabilization mechanism for the yuan's exchange rate and a pledge to reach an agreement on the protection of intellectual property rights. A target was set for presidents Donald Trump and Xi Jinping to sign the deal by the end of the year. "We have made substantial progress in many fields. We are happy about it. We'll continue to make efforts," declared Deputy Prime Minister and chief Chinese negotiator Liu He at an Oval Office appearance with Donald Trump. US officials were less optimistic. "I think we have a fundamental understanding on the key issues. We've gone through a significant amount of paper, but there is more work to do," said US Treasury Secretary Steven Mnuchin. Meanwhile, US Trade Representative Robert Lighthizer, a key player in the negotiations, warned China that Trump had made no decisions about the other tariff increases planned for December.[6]

---

[6]In another sign of the stiffening attitude of the American administration towards China, the State Department issued a directive on October 16, 2019, urging all Chinese diplomats present on American soil to submit advance notification of their meetings with US officials, as well as with academic and research institutions. It highlighted that the move was a simple measure of reciprocity inasmuch as American diplomats are subject to the same restrictions in their work in China. Beijing responded immediately, with its embassy in Washington declaring that the measure violated the Vienna Convention (Chinese diplomats, 2019). Furthermore, the US Interior Department, on October 31, 2019, grounded its Chinese-made drones,

Washington and Beijing finally reached a commercial truce on December 13, 2019, when they agreed upon the terms of Phase 1 and indicated that it was to be part of a larger Phase 2 agreement, the negotiations for which had yet to be started. Under the terms of this truce, the United States agreed to suspend a series of tariffs on Chinese products (mainly cell phones, personal computers, toys, clothing, automobiles) in exchange for China's commitment to purchase $200 billion worth of American products in 2020 and 2021, including $40 billion per year of agricultural goods. President Donald Trump signed the agreement on January 15, 2020. However, Chinese resentment was very strong, as the remarks made by State Councilor and Foreign Minister Wang Yi on November 23, 2019, at the meeting of G20 Foreign Ministers in Nagoya (Japan) testified. The United States had "become the world's biggest destabilizing factor", he said on the sidelines of the meeting. "The United States is broadly engaged in unilateralism and protectionism, and is damaging multilateralism and the multilateral trading system." And in a highly unusual public accusation from a senior Chinese official, he said, "Certain US politicians have smeared China everywhere in the world, but have not produced any evidence."

The awakening on both sides of the Pacific Ocean has been brutal and painful, as Jonathan Holslag, professor of international politics at the Free University of Brussels and author of *China's Coming War with Asia* (2015), chronicles in his regular columns in *Le Monde*. In one of his more recent pieces, he commented:

> Until recently, the prevailing view in the United States was that China could be converted to Western manners, that the "Washington consensus", with its imperatives of liberalism and privatization, would be slowly but surely

---

suspecting they may pose a national security risk. The department had 810 drones, of which 786 were manufactured in China. Chinese company Da Jiang Innovations (DJI), based in Shenzhen, is the world number one in drones with 70% of the market. The US army had led the way, a few months earlier, by deciding to ban Chinese-built drones it suspected of transmitting to China sensitive digital data, such as location, images and video recordings.

adopted by Beijing. China would open up to Western companies and trade flows would re-balance. The growth of China would not threaten the security of the West as long as the liberal values of the international order remained the same... Some were skeptical, but they were told that there was no other option but to try to take China down this path. But this prospect, despite a huge investment in different forums for international dialog and an almost complete opening of the Western market to China, has not materialized... The Obama administration already understood this, but it was Donald Trump who resolved to stop what the Americans now see as a predatory strategy. In essence, Washington now considers that China must be stopped economically before it becomes a military threat. (Holslag, 2019)

In its economic war with America, China has an important asset that can serve as a powerful means of retaliation: rare earths. The name covers seventeen metallic elements (lanthanum, cerium, praseodymium, neodymium, promethium, samarium, europium, gadolinium, terbium, dysprosium, holmium, erbium, thulium, ytterbium, lutetium, scandium and yttrium) with desirable electronic, catalytic, magnetic and optical properties. They have become indispensable in the automotive, aeronautics, defense and high-tech sectors. They are present in magnets, flat screens, smartphones, tablets, electric car batteries, wind turbines, catalytic converters, solar panels and even radars. "Holmium is used to make control bars in the nuclear industry, microwaves... neodymium is used to make very strong magnets, to make robots, cars, hard drives, and wind turbines," said Juan Diego Rodriguez-Blanco, a mineralogy professor at Trinity College Dublin. (Sanchez Manzanaro, 2019) Rare earths are also used in the aerospace and military industries for manufacturing hardened glass, fuel additives and lasers. In addition to high-tech applications, they are also necessary for medical research as well as in certain treatments for lung, prostate and bone cancer.

Despite their critical importance for Western economies, China currently controls almost all of the global market for rare earths. Of the 170,000 tons produced in 2018, China produced 71% (120,000 tons) according to the US Geological Survey. The other major producers (Australia, 20,000 tons, and the United States, 15,000 tons) were far behind. The United States was once one of the biggest producers of rare earths, which despite their name are not rare and can be found throughout the world. Today the United States is almost 80% dependent upon Chinese imports. Beijing has not only threatened to wield this economic weapon to obtain political goals, it has used it. In 2010, China suddenly suspended its rare earths deliveries to Japan to obtain the release of a Chinese fishing vessel accused of having collided with two Japanese patrol boats off the Senkaku Islands (also claimed by Beijing, which calls them the Diaoyu Islands). Overnight, dozens of Japanese high-tech businesses ceased to receive shipments of rare earths, which gave rise to a whiff of panic across the archipelago. As Guillaume Pitron, a French journalist and author who specializes in the geopolitics of raw materials, has noted:

> For Beijing, this below the belt punch on rare metals was first and foremost a question of survival. Along with the United States, China is the country most concerned about the security of its supplies… Beijing quickly understood the leverage and power that this stranglehold on rare metals gave it… China is very reluctant to provide certain production data, which it considers as state secrets. There are hidden stocks, geostrategic factors, diplomatic considerations that make reading the markets particularly difficult, even for the best specialists. (Pitron, 2018: 118, 121)

In May 2019, President Xi Jinping and his Deputy Prime Minister and chief negotiator Liu He visited the site of JL Mag Rare-Earth, a leading rare earths producer located in the southeastern province of Jiangxi. The message was crystal clear: remind the United States and the world that China controls these strategic metals.

Faced with this situation, the United States could not stand idly by. In July 2019, Donald Trump transmitted to the Secretary of Defense five memorandums in which he declared the production of rare earth metals as "essential to the national defense". In December of the same year, the US army announced its intention to finance the construction of facilities for the mining and processing of rare earths to ensure there was a domestic supply chain for elements critical for military use. Texas Mineral Company Resources Corp. and USA Rare Earth announced soon afterward the construction of a pilot processing plant in Colorado, which launched operations in July 2020. The goal is to eventually build a larger installation near Round Top mountain in West Texas, which alone could supply the United States with almost all of its rare earths needs for decades to come, and which also has large deposits of lithium needed for batteries for electric vehicles.

Chapter 3

The Great Partition of the World: Geostrategic Competition

Russia is Beijing's new ally. Africa has become a new Chinese colony where Beijing has become the dominant political and economic influence there at the expense of the old colonial powers. Latin America is a new target. Far East Asia is still allied with the United States. Japan is a bulwark against Chinese expansion. South Korea is another crucial link in the US military's deployment. Taiwan, while unrecognized diplomatically, is a strategic element in US policy for the Asia-Pacific region. North Korea remains in the Chinese orbit. India is the other Asian giant and China's great rival. Southeast Asia is soon to be China's economic preserve. The Middle East is at boiling point. In this kid-glove confrontation, Europe is trying to somehow maintain its unity and independence in the face of Chinese and American appetites.

"As the United States withdraws from the rest of the world, China quickly occupies the smallest space that becomes available."

Steen Jakobsen
Chief Economist at Saxo Bank

Donald Trump pulled the United States out of international agreements. It started just three days after his inauguration as president. On January 23, 2017, he pulled the US out of the Trans-Pacific Partnership (TPP) Agreement, a multilateral free-trade agreement signed the previous year to integrate the economies of the Asia-Pacific and Americas regions. The TPP would have brought together the United States, Canada, Mexico, Chile, Peru, Japan, Malaysia, Vietnam, Singapore, Brunei, Australia and New Zealand, an area comprising 800 million inhabitants and 40% of global GDP, making it the largest free trade zone in the world. This spectacular withdrawal generated a shock wave among America's allies in the region, who saw it as a worrying sign of America's disengagement. The other countries nevertheless went ahead and in March 2018 concluded another agreement: the Comprehensive and Progressive Agreement for Trans-Pacific Partnership (CPTPP). The United States also pulled out from the UN Human Rights Council, UNESCO, the Joint Comprehensive Plan of Action (JCPOA) on Iran's nuclear program, the Paris Agreement on climate change and global warming and other international agreements. It also withdrew its funding for the United Nations Relief and Works Agency for Palestine Refugees (UNRWA). And while the United States remained a member of the World Trade Organization, Trump paralyzed the WTO dispute resolution mechanism by blocking the appointment of appellate judges.

Meanwhile, China's profile on the international scene has risen, and its influence over much of the planet has grown.[1] Beijing has been at pains to reassure the world its intentions are benign. Speaking on the sidelines of the UN General Assembly in New York in September 2019, Chinese Foreign Minister Wang Yi said "seeking hegemony is not in our DNA" and that "China has no intention to play the Game of Thrones on the world stage." (*China says*, 2019) In an August 2020 interview with the Xinhua news agency, which was uncharacteristically published in full, Wang said China had no intention to replace the United States as a global superpower. He said China did not want a

---

[1] In his book *The Rise of the Trading State: Commerce in the Modern World*, American economist Richard Rosecrance (1986) explained that after the Second World War, the great powers established their power mainly thanks to trade, commercial surpluses, direct investment, technology transfers and the accumulation of foreign capital, and not by territorial expansion.

cold war with the United States but acknowledged their relations were in the "most complex situation" in 40 years. "Today's China is not the former Soviet Union. We have no intention of becoming another United States. China does not export ideology, and never interferes in other countries' internal affairs," said Wang. While these remarks sound reassuring, some of China's actions attest to the contrary.

The face-off between China and the United States still does not seem like a fair fight in the strategic and military sphere. America has forged multiple alliances across the world while China has no friends except perhaps Pakistan and North Korea. And China's links with the North Korean "hermit kingdom" are more of a burden than an advantage. In 2017, the United States had a total of 800 military bases in 177 countries spread over five continents. These held almost 200,000 soldiers, or 10% of American military personnel. At the same time, China had only one foreign base, in Djibouti, which was inaugurated in August 2017. The opening of a second military base in Cambodia is said to be under discussion. The Ream naval base in the Gulf of Thailand would be made available to the Chinese military. Cambodian authorities have denied such reports. A third Chinese military base in the Pacific was in the works following a September 2019 agreement reached between the state company China Sam Group[2] and the government of the Solomon Islands to rent the small island of Tulagi which has a deep water mooring suitable for naval facilities. (Lavallée, 2019) The island previously served as a naval base for the Japanese fleet during World War II. But a month later the government of the Solomon Islands suddenly backtracked and canceled the deal, presumably due to American diplomatic pressure.

It is often said that China has no friends. This is no longer quite true because it has forged a brand-new alliance with Russia, its immense neighbor with which the rapprochement has been appreciable since 2014. This has clearly accelerated as Sino-American tensions rose, to

---

[2] China Sam Group operates in multiple business areas, from gas exploitation to the security sector. One of its subsidiaries, China Jing An, was formerly part of the Ministry of Public Security.

the point that some observers are now talking of a new honeymoon between Beijing and Moscow. Since coming to power, Xi Jinping has visited Russia six times and met Vladimir Putin on about 20 occasions in total. At the same time, Sino-Russian economic cooperation is diversifying and now includes projects of strategic importance for the national development of both countries. Xi Jinping does not miss an opportunity to stress that Vladimir Putin is "his best friend".[3]

This new friendship between the two countries, sealed by the signing in 2001 of a treaty on "Good-Neighborliness, Friendship and Cooperation", is visible in joint military maneuvers and significant cooperation in the area of space. In October 2019, Vladimir Putin took a further step in the Sino-Russian military alliance with the announcement that Russia will provide China with a new ultra-sophisticated warning system against intercontinental ballistic missile attacks.

"Our friendship and our work together are not aimed against anybody," declared the Russian president… "This is a very serious thing that will drastically enhance the defensive capacity of the People's Republic of China as currently only the US and Russia have such systems." (*Russia helping China*, 2019)

It is a remark that targets the United States, according to Beijing-based military analyst Zhou Chenming, who believes the new system will eventually cover Beijing, Tianjin, Hebei Province, the Yangtze Delta and the Greater Bay Area in southern China, as well as areas in central China.

Economic links have also grown significantly closer in recent years. Russian-Chinese trade broke the $108 billion mark in 2018, and the

---

[3] In 2001, Vladimir Putin actively contributed to the creation of the Shanghai Cooperation Organization (SCO), which initially included China, Kazakhstan, Kyrgyzstan, Russia, Tajikistan and Uzbekistan, as a step in the creation of a non-Western alliance. India and Pakistan joined the SCO in 2017. In 2015, Putin played a key role in the creation of the Eurasian Economic Union (EAEU) and signed an agreement with Xi Jinping later that year on the "harmonization" of the EAEU and the Belt and Road Initiative (BRI).

nations aim for it to reach $200 billion in the near future. A recent illustration of Sino-Russian rapprochement in this sphere is the inauguration by Vladimir Putin and Xi Jinping in December 2019 of the 2,000-kilometer gas pipeline called "Power of Siberia". It is the first of its kind linking Russia's gas deposits in Eastern Siberia to the Chinese border. But this new alliance has quickly shown that it is constrained by the economic weakness of Russia compared to its partner, the structural imbalance of bilateral trade in favor of China, the demographic disparity along their border of more than three thousand kilometers, and mutual distrust fed by an antagonistic common past. These factors work to undermine this new rapprochement. As it stands today, this relationship is that of a dominant country, which is clearly China, and a dominated country, Russia. While Putin once lamented the collapse of the Soviet Union in 1991 as "the greatest geopolitical catastrophe of the century", he is realistic about Russia's standing in the world. He has even publicly recognized the economic and military primacy of the United States. At the Saint Petersburg International Economic Forum in June 2016, he declared: "America is a great power — today probably the only superpower. We accept that." (Putin says accepts, 2016)

China has expanded its economic influence in Africa, Southeast Asia and even in Latin America since the late 1990s, imposing itself as a dominant player. In Africa, Beijing has almost completely pushed out the French and British, the former colonial powers, making the continent its new sphere of influence. China started by increasing the amount of its financial development assistance for African countries. Its trade with Africa went from $10.8 billion in 2001 to $166 billion in 2011 and $170 billion in 2017, according to the Chinese commerce ministry. China imports from Africa oil, minerals and timber, and exports consumer goods, drugs, machinery and vehicles. France has gradually been ousted from Africa's markets. According to Coface (a French foreign trade insurance company), the market share of French exports in Africa has halved since 2000, dropping from 11% to 5.5% in 2017, while China's market share went from 3% to 18%. Meanwhile, the public debt of sub-Saharan Africa countries shot up 40% in three years to stand at 45% of their GDP at the end of 2017, with China the leading creditor. According to the World Bank, in 2018 there were approximately one million Chinese workers on African soil, employed in various tasks such as retail, agriculture and construction. The same institution indicated that investments by Chinese financial institutions in Africa increased from $1 billion a year before 2004 to $7 billion in 2006. Chinese financial aid has also exploded, with aid from China's Exim Bank totaling $67.2 billion between 2001 and 2010, compared to $54.7 billion granted by the World Bank during this period.

These exchanges have facilitated closer political and diplomatic relations, especially with countries that previously supported Taiwan. China has established them on the basis of the close relations it once had with developing countries, in the 1960s and 1970s, as a "big brother". China, unlike Western countries, turns a blind eye to the human rights situation when it grants aid. The second most visible aspect of the Chinese presence in Africa is the plethora of contracts for infrastructure projects (railways, roads, ports, airports). Chinese companies account for around 40% of all projects financed by the World Bank. During a tour in August 2012, then US Secretary of State Hillary Clinton denounced a "new economic colonialism" in Africa, without mentioning China by name. During a visit to Ethiopia in May 2014, Chinese Prime Minister Li Keqiang stressed that "China will never pursue a policy of colonialism as some countries have." But there is another side of the coin: African countries are having great difficulty repaying their Chinese lenders. The example of Kenya is striking. The repayment of interest on Kenyan debt to China accounted for 87.1% of the total interest owed to all of its lenders during the year to June 2019, compared with 81% the previous year. (Munda, 2019) As of June 2019, Chinese loans represented 66.4% of Kenya's total debt.

China's presence in Africa is also felt through a propaganda offensive and by the entry in force of Chinese media into the continent's audio-visual markets. First by CGTN Africa, a subsidiary of Chinese state television, which never talks about corruption or human rights. It kept silent about the massive debate over corruption in the construction of the Standard Gauge Railway (SGR), the new railway line connecting

Nairobi and Mombasa inaugurated in 2017. On the contrary, CGTN Africa presented this project as a positive illustration of Sino-African relations: harmonious and "win-win". Beijing has also launched the *China Daily Africa* and the English-language monthly *ChinAfrica*. But Africans find their content boring. (China is broadening, 2018) Beijing has developed a massive training program for African journalists in China, with a thousand scholarships every year. Taking advantage of its economic ties, China now wields significant political influence over many of its African partners. This is how China ensured in October 2014 that South Africa refused the Dalai Lama a visa to attend a Nobel Peace Prize Summit in Cape Town.[4] Faced with this refusal, the other participants canceled the summit. Pretoria's position provoked the anger of former South African archbishop Desmond Tutu, the Nobel Peace Prize laureate in 1984, who said he was "ashamed" to see his country "bow down" before China. However, we should not overestimate the Chinese presence in Africa, according to sinologist Jean-Pierre Cabestan, a professor at Hong Kong Baptist University and a specialist in China-Africa relations. "The Chinese presence in Africa is first of all visible. It is essential for African countries. China is everywhere in Africa. Its presence is economic, political and even military. There isn't an African country where China isn't present. But African countries have a lot of partners. The former colonial powers, the United States, the other emerging countries setting up shop in Africa, in particular Turkey: the game is fairly open."[5]

Japan is trying, with limited success, to compete with China in Africa. This is why Tokyo promised 300 billion yen ($2.75 Billion at the average 2019 exchange) in help during the 7th Tokyo International Conference on African Development (TICAD) which gathered 54 African leaders in Yokohama in August 2019. The Japanese government founded TICAD in 1993 with the ambition of boosting trade with Africa, in particular to obtain the raw materials its industry needs. Ten years later, China created its own Forum on

---

[4] The Tibetan spiritual leader Dalai Lama won the Nobel Peace Prize in 1989.
[5] Interview with the author, October 4, 2019.

China-Africa Cooperation. China-Africa trade reached $204 billion in 2018, up by 20% from 2017. By contrast, trade between Africa and Japan is very modest, with Japan's exports to the African continent amounting to $7.8 billion and its imports totaling $8.7 billion in 2017. On the sidelines of the TICAD, the head of the Djibouti port authority and free trade zone, Aboubaker Omar Hadi, told the Japanese business daily *Nikkei* that it had "*no other choice*" than to go to China to find financing for $11 billion in investments needed to modernize the infrastructure of the Horn of Africa enclave. The new Djibouti free trade zone, which opened in 2018, is already 40% controlled by Chinese capital. The port is strategically located along a sea corridor connecting Africa to the rest of the world.

In Asia, the Chinese presence has grown significantly these past years. At $8.3 billion in 2017, China is fourth in terms of foreign direct investment into Asia (not including Hong Kong), behind the European Union ($22.2 billion), Japan ($20.1 billion), and the United States ($13.6 billion). It is ahead of South Korea and Australia, as well as Hong Kong. Including Hong Kong puts China at $12.8 billion and on the heels of the United States. China's economic and political ties with the 11 Southeast Asian countries are very developed. Starting at the end of the 1990s, the rapprochement accelerated considerably from 2001. The entry into force of the China-ASEAN[6] free trade zone in 2010 was a major step in further deepening ties. Several ASEAN countries and others such as Cambodia and Nepal are now completely in the Chinese orbit.

In Cambodia, one of the poorest countries in the world, the Chinese presence is overwhelming. Chinese merchants arrived by the hundreds of thousands to take control of the workings of the local economy in cities like Sihanoukville. It was a small, peaceful fishing port in the south of the country until 2017, when the Chinese arrived in droves,

---

[6]Founded in 1967, the Association of Southeast Asian Nations (ASEAN) includes Brunei, Burma, Cambodia, Indonesia, Laos, Malaysia, the Philippines, Singapore, Thailand and Vietnam. The member countries have 620 million inhabitants and a GDP of $2.400 trillion.

taking advantage of an easing in the immigration rules. The population is now reaching 90,000, of which 80,000 are Chinese, and Mandarin can be heard spoken everywhere. Almost 90% of businesses are in Chinese hands: hotels, casinos (there are 88 in the city compared to 5 in 2015), restaurants, massage parlors, brothels, according to Chuon Narin, the police chief for Preah Sihanouk province. The influx of the Chinese has been accompanied by new scourges denounced by the indigenous population: illicit gambling, prostitution, drug trafficking, and money laundering. Cambodia has become a popular tourist destination for the Chinese, with 1.9 million tourists visiting in 2018 against 1.2 million in 2017. Many Chinese immigrants settled in Sihanoukville to take advantage of a legal system that is more flexible than in China. "Back in the Chinese mainland, the local authorities have a stronger capacity and capability to enforce law and order," said Neak Chandarith, head of international studies at the University of Phnom Penh. "But the small group of Chinese who have come to Sihanoukville are not investors. They've come here to take advantage of the weak capacity and capability [in law enforcement]… That is the problem now." Alex Gonzalez-Davidson, an activist from the NGO Mother Nature Cambodia, is worried that "Sihanoukville could become a major hub for the laundering of dirty money from China, mainly through the totally unregulated gambling and property sectors." (Huang, 2019)

In Nepal, instruction is now conducted in Chinese in many secondary schools. The Tibetan refugees trying to cross the border with Nepal to reach India are systematically stopped and handed over to the Chinese police. On July 8, 2019, the official celebrations of the 84th birthday of the Dalai Lama in the small Himalayan country where the Buddha[7] was born, were abruptly canceled upon the order of Beijing. Myanmar, which also jealously guards its independence, has become considerably closer to China, to which it offers a precious opening onto the Indian Ocean and access to its rich natural resources.

---

[7] Siddhartha Gautama, the Buddha, was born in 623 BC in the famous Lumbini Gardens in southern Nepal, near the border with India.

China concluded a common defense pact with Malaysia in 2005, which provides for the exchange of information in the military field and greater cooperation in the defense industry. This rapprochement was reinforced in April 2017 with the establishment of a high-level committee on bilateral military relations. The Chinese navy also started conducting joint patrols with the Vietnamese navy in the Gulf of Tonkin in 2003, despite disputes over islands in the South China Sea. With the Philippines, relations have developed largely to the detriment of the United States since the coming to power of Rodrigo Duterte as president in 2016, despite their territorial dispute over islands. Annual military discussions with the Philippines that had been frozen since 2013 were resumed in 2017. China has not stopped since the start of the 2010s to deepen, with relative success, security ties with its ASEAN neighbors. But China's military expansionism in the South China Sea and its growing influence in the Asia-Pacific region are cause for growing concern for the countries there, allowing the United States to consolidate its influence with its partners in the area.

In the 2000s the United States began a quiet but real rapprochement with India, which is the sworn enemy of Pakistan and great rival of China, whose rise in power in the Asia-Pacific region New Delhi fears above all else. The first step in this process was the visit to New Delhi in March 2006 by President George W. Bush, who then granted India the possibility to buy American civilian nuclear technology. The second step was the signing in September 2018, during a visit to New Delhi by Secretary of State Mike Pompeo and Defense Secretary Jim Mattis, of the Comcasa Agreement (Communications Compatibility and Security Agreement), which paved the way for US arms sales to India and the exchange of sensitive military data. The two countries also agreed to conduct joint land, naval and air military exercises in 2019. America agreed in particular to provide India with information on Chinese troop movements along the Sino-Indian border. India has not forgotten the crushing defeat it suffered in 1962 at the hands of China in a brief border conflict. The fighting did not resolve the disputes between Beijing and New Delhi. And while the border had been quiet for years, a clash broke out on June 15, 2020, in the Galwan Valley, which runs along the border of India's Ladakh region and the Aksai Chin region that China annexed in 1962. The fighting with clubs and stones left 20 Indian soldiers dead. China has never released a toll. Both have denied responsibility for the fighting and moved more troops to the area, where further skirmishes took place during the summer and into the autumn. The incidents, the first fighting along the Himalayan border since 1975, have led India to cool its relations with China. While it is unlikely to push India into the arms of the United States, the incident is likely to affect Chinese-Indian relations for years to come.

The third step in the US-India rapprochement was the visit to the United States of Indian Prime Minister Narendra Modi in September 2019. Modi was welcomed with open arms by Donald Trump at a giant meeting in Houston, Texas, organized in his honor by the Indian diaspora. This event, which brought together more than 50,000 Americans, many of Indian origin, was billed as the biggest reception ever for a foreign leader in the United States except for the Pope. Donald Trump had his eyes riveted on the next election and the weight of the voters of the Indian diaspora, who represent 1% of the US population. Today, India, the most populous democracy in the world, and the United States, the oldest democracy in the world, are looking at each other in the eye and weighing their shared strategic interests. India remains concerned about its independence and there is no question of it becoming a vassal of the United States. On the other hand, for the United States, Pakistan remains an important ally, especially in the struggle against radical Islamism. Finally, India has been seeking, since Narendra Modi's visit to China in April 2018, to calm its tumultuous relations with Beijing. Already, to please Beijing, restrictions have been imposed by the government of India on contacts between its ministers and the Dalai Lama, who has resided since 1959 in Dharamsala, in the north of India.

Over the years, China has also succeeded in gradually extracting Nepal from India's sphere of influence to its own. This culminated with Xi Jinping's visit to Kathmandu in October 2019 when China and Nepal greeted the birth of a "new era" in their relationship, with Beijing promising 3.5 billion yuan ($526 million[8]) in aid over the 2020–2022 period. Furthermore, China pledged to assist Nepal if necessary to "safeguard its sovereignty", a first in the history of Chinese diplomacy. Nepal, on the other hand, ceded to Chinese pressure and concluded an extradition treaty which mainly targets Tibetans seeking exile who cross over the border of this small Himalayan republic where 20,000 Tibetan refugees live.

China has long maintained friendly relations with Pakistan. Official texts, declarations, and speeches proclaim that China and Pakistan are united in a "deep" friendship that is "sweeter than honey" and "unbreakable" and which has "withstood the test of time". According to Mathieu Duchâtel, a researcher at the Stockholm International Peace Research Institute (SIPRI), the "all-weather friendship" between China and Pakistan was "born of the common interest to contain Indian power". (Dall'Orso, 2016) Beijing secretly helped its Pakistani ally to develop nuclear weapons. Islamabad and Beijing opened diplomatic relations in 1950 when Pakistan broke with Taiwan and recognized the People's Republic of China as the only legitimate representative of China. It was the first Muslim country to do so. According to *The New York Times*, Beijing and Islamabad agreed at the end of 2018 to set up a military alliance along the China-Pakistan Economic Corridor (CPEC) under construction (3,000 kilometers of roads, railways, oil and gas pipelines requiring some $62 billion in investments) which will provide a link from western China to the Arabian Sea close to the Persian Gulf.[9]

The two countries have also reportedly moved forward on a "secret proposal" to equip the Pakistani air force with Chinese-built "military jets, weaponry and other hardware". The project includes plans to deepen the cooperation between the two nations in space, according to *The New York Times*. The newspaper said the military projects were later included as part of China's Belt and Road Initiative, despite repeated

---

[8] Unless otherwise stated, currency conversions are conducted at the rate as of November 22, 2020.

[9] See Chapter 6 — The New Silk Road.

declarations by Beijing that it is purely an economic project with peaceful intent. (Abi-Habib, 2018) Just before his official visit to India in October 2019, Xi Jinping took care to welcome Pakistani Prime Minister Imran Khan for a two-day state visit. China has backed its Pakistani ally on the painful Kashmir issue. For seventy years India and Pakistan have disputed the border region which they both claim and partially occupy. Pakistan has long wanted international mediation to settle what is one of the longest-running border disputes in the world, but India categorically refuses. For New Delhi, it is a matter of national sovereignty.

The island of Taiwan, also called the Republic of China and formerly Formosa, is a geostrategic issue of prime importance for the United States in the Asia-Pacific region. It is the queen of the political chess-board of the region, a bulwark against Chinese influence that Washington cannot lose at any cost. This is why the United States is the leading supplier of military equipment to the Republic of China. Taiwan's population of 23 million inhabitants is 93% Han Chinese and is by a large majority hostile to reunification with the Chinese main-land. A Japanese colony between 1895 and 1945, Taiwan represents the last link in the reunification of the Chinese nation under the leadership of the Chinese Communist Party after the "peaceful liberation" of Tibet in 1950 and the return to Chinese sovereignty of Hong Kong in 1997 and Macao in 1999. According to a survey carried out in March 2019 on behalf of the Taiwanese government's Mainland Affairs Council, eight out of ten of the island's inhabitants oppose reunification. While more than isolated on the diplomatic level (only 15 countries still had diplomatic relations with the island at the beginning of 2020), Taiwan has its own government, army and all the political attributes of an independent state. Under the Taiwan Relations Act, adopted in April 1979, the United States pledged to grant the island military aid so that it can defend itself. The act states that "the United States will make available to Taiwan such defense articles and defense services in such quantity as may be necessary to enable Taiwan to maintain a sufficient self-defense capability." Although it recognized the People's Republic of China in January 1979, Washington has its "American Institute" in

Taipei, an unofficial embassy through which bilateral relations are mostly conducted. This office, in which more than 450 people work, represents American interests in the areas of trade, agriculture, consular services and cultural exchanges. In January 2020, Tsai Ing-wen, a bête noire of Beijing as she is deeply hostile to a reunification of the island with the Communist mainland, was re-elected for a second four-year term as president.[10] She easily beat her rival from the Kuomintang, Han Kuo-yu, who was more open to the idea of compromise with Beijing. Since her reelection, Tsai has made some progress in breaking the island's diplomatic isolation. Several unprecedented official contacts with US officials have taken place, in particular the September 2020 visit by Under Secretary of State for Economic Growth, Energy, and the Environment Keith Krach. He was the highest-ranking US diplomatic official to visit Taiwan in 41 years, and he was naturally received by Tsai. Krach's visit was preceded in August by the visit of Health Secretary Alex Azar and then followed in December by Environmental Protection Agency Administrator Andrew Wheeler, who also has cabinet secretary rank.

Japan, which has the world's third-largest economy, is for its part a close ally of the United States. Its relations with China are tumultuous, mainly due to memories of the atrocities committed by the Japanese imperial army during the Sino-Japanese war from 1937 to 1945 that left at least 20 million Chinese dead.[11] Japan has expressed its "regrets", but China, as well as South Korea, another country colonized by Japan, are still waiting for a formal apology. Beijing skillfully uses these dark pages from history to influence Japanese politics,

---

[10] At the end of November 2019, the Chinese spy Wang Liqiang defected and requested political asylum in Australia. On November 23, he had told the Australian daily The Age about his activities as a spy for the PRC in Hong Kong and in Taiwan, such as training agents and infiltrating Taiwanese political circles with the goal of sabotaging Tsai Ing-wen's election.

[11] A particularly murderous episode was the sacking of Nanking in December 1937. The Japanese army entered the city and committed massacres on a large scale: executions with bayonets, swords or machine guns; rapes and mutilations. At least 100,000 people were killed, with the Chinese authorities putting their official toll at 300,000.

accusing Tokyo of not having totally disavowed its past. The repeated visits between 2001 and 2006 by Japanese Prime Minister Junichiro Koizumi to the Yasukuni shrine in Tokyo, which houses the souls of the country's war dead, including some convicted of war crimes, were flash points of tension between the two countries. The willingness of his successor, Shinzo Abe, to reform Japan's constitution also raises questions in China. Drafted by the Americans, the constitution entered into force in 1947 and prohibits Japan from resorting to war to settle international disputes. A territorial dispute over the Senkaku Islands has also aggravated Sino-Japanese relations. Nevertheless, Japan is by far China's most important trade partner in Asia, accounting for 15% of China's imports. China, for its part, became in the 2000s Japan's largest trade partner, taking the place of the United States. For a long time, Japan was the main supplier of official development assistance to China. From 1979, when Japan gave its first public aid to China, to 2005, Tokyo provided nearly $26.5 billion to the country. Since the end of the 2000s, an evolution has taken shape with Japanese business leaders becoming enthusiastic investors on the Chinese mainland.

The strategic rapprochement between the United States and Japan remains for China an additional element of mistrust of its neighbor. Japan is itself worried about the rise of China in Asia and its huge increase in military spending. For the United States, Japan today represents a crucial bulwark against China. Japan has been linked with the United States by a security treaty since 1960. More than 45,000 American soldiers are stationed in the archipelago. Japan has an ultra-modern navy that counterbalances the Chinese naval presence in East Asia. Yet Japan is a vulnerable country. It lacks most of the energy resources it needs, importing 100% of the oil that is vital for its economy and its people. Some 127 million Japanese live in an area of just 377,944 km2 (145,925 square miles) for an average density of 336 inhabitants per square kilometer, although the population is heavily concentrated in urban spaces. Faced with these security, demographic and economic challenges, Japan very quickly after WWII found in the United States its natural ally.

China, on the other hand, maintains close relations with the city-state of Singapore, which emerged as an independent nation in August 1965 when it was expelled by Malaysia. Singapore has an important Chinese community that accounts for 75% of the population and which has forged strong cultural and economic exchanges with China. Many Singaporean students choose to go to China to continue their studies. The "father" of the nation of Singapore, Lee Kuan Yew, developed close relations with the Chinese leadership, to whom he provided much political advice. Singapore, however, remains marked by the sustained desire of successive governments to fight against the influence of communism on the capitalist island, which today maintains polite relations with China against a backdrop of robust trade. Singapore-China relations have strengthened since the 2000s, with the first joint maneuvers of the Singapore Armed Forces and the People's Liberation Army being held in 2014. Many Chinese from the mainland have migrated to Singapore since the 1990s. With their numbers increasing, so has their ability to wield pressure.

Finally, China has had close economic ties with Australia even though it is an ally of the United States and is an important piece for Washington on the geostrategic chessboard that stretches from the Americas to the Asia-Pacific region. However, suspicion reigns in Canberra over recent Chinese attempts to influence Australian politics. In 2015, Australian intelligence was amazed to discover that all of the nation's political parties were being actively funded by generous donors who were agents of the Chinese Communist Party. China has little by little penetrated Australian universities and research centers to siphon off technologies. Seduction, flattery, money, threats or even coercion: the Australian press has revealed that thousands of Chinese agents have infiltrated public life and the upper echelons of the country's civil service. Beijing's number one goal is to undermine the alliance between Australia and the United States. In political circles, warnings against the increasing interference from China in Australia's internal affairs continue to multiply.

Andrew Hastie, head of the Australian parliament's Joint Committee on Intelligence and Security, has asserted that China has been secretly interfering in his country's media, universities and politics. Hastie drew the ire of colleagues with an August 2019 opinion piece that criticized China's authoritarian rise and likened complacency about Xi Jinping's philosophy and intentions to Europe's response to Nazi Germany before World War II. The strong Chinese presence in all sectors of Australia's economy led to Parliament adopting at the end of June 2019 a series of laws to fight against espionage and foreign interference. One of them aims to prohibit international donations to political parties so that they do not serve foreign strategic interests. It follows the case of Labor Senator Sam Dastyari who received donations in 2018 from a wealthy Chinese man and who then took a stand in favor of Chinese territorial claims in the South China Sea. Meanwhile, China has indicted on espionage charges a 54-year-old Chinese-born Australian, Yang Hengjun. The former diplomat turned writer, academic and businessman was detained in January 2019.

Relations between China and Australia continued to deteriorate in 2020. Canberra provoked Beijing's ire in the spring by publicly calling for an international inquiry into the COVID-19 pandemic. Beijing then slapped tariffs on Australian barley, blocked beef imports from four slaughterhouses, and turned a cold shoulder to Australian officials who sought consultations. The moves could trigger a rethink of Australia's decades-long economic reliance on China, which buys nearly a third of the country's exports and is its biggest trading partner by far. In August, Chinese authorities arrested Cheng Lei, a Chinese-born Australian who worked for Chinese state TV network CGTN as an anchor for its English-language service. Then, in September, the last two Australian journalists in China, Bill Birtles of the Australian Broadcasting Corporation (ABC) and Michael Smith of the Australian Financial Review (AFR), were forced to make a hasty exit after risks rose they could be detained.

North Korea is a close but highly problematic ally for China. In June 2016, on the occasion of a rare official visit by Xi Jinping to Pyongyang, North Korean leader Kim Jong-un said the relationship between the two countries was "invincible" and their friendship "immutable". The neighboring countries have been linked by a treaty of friendship, cooperation and mutual assistance since July 1961, which was signed by then prime minister Zhou Enlai and North Korean dictator Kim Il-sung. During the Korean War (1950–1953), China intervened on the side of the North by sending 500,000 soldiers to face off against South Korean and US forces. China is the first and pretty much the sole economic partner of North Korea. Chinese imports constitute an economic infusion that is essential to the survival of the North Korean regime. China provides 90% of North Korea's energy supplies, 80% of its manufactured goods and 45% of its food. Despite their ideological proximity, Beijing has only very limited influence on the policy pursued by Pyongyang. China has failed to put an end to the nuclear tests conducted by its neighbor, as well as its launches of ballistic missiles. China has wearily approved each of the 12 United Nations Security Council resolutions imposing tougher sanctions against North Korea since 1993.

The alliance with this now cumbersome ally has not prevented Beijing from forging close relations with South Korea, a country with which it established diplomatic relations in August 1992. Xi Jinping's visit to Seoul in May 2019 illustrated Beijing's desire to maintain a balance between the two rivals on the Korean peninsula. South Korea's spectacular economic development has further strengthened links with China. But South Korea remains a close ally of the United States, with which it concluded a mutual defense treaty in 1953. Some 29,000 American soldiers are stationed on South Korean soil. The South Korean and US armed forces conduct joint military maneuvers every year, brushing aside North Korean protests. South Korea, Japan and the United States are linked by an agreement on sharing military intelligence concerning North Korea as well as China, known as GSOMIA (General Security of Military Information Agreement).

Latin America may be in the United States' geographical backyard, but it has in recent years become another playground for Beijing. Although historically there has been little contact between their civilizations and cultures, trade between the two is increasing at a staggering rate. China provided, between 2005 and 2014, more than $100 billion in loans to Latin American businesses, according to the Inter-American

Dialogue, an American think tank. During roughly the same period the two main banks in China, China Development Bank and China Exim Bank, alone financed projects totaling $102.2 billion in the region, according to the China-Latin America Finance Database. Meanwhile, the volume of trade in goods between China and the Latin America-Caribbean region (LAC) went from almost zero in 1990 to $10 billion in 2000, then soared to $266 billion in 2017, according to the UN's Economic Commission for Latin America and the Caribbean, matching US trade with countries in the region. By 2016, China had become the top or second-largest trading partner of Argentina, Bolivia, Brazil, Chile, Colombia, Ecuador and Peru. China has also become the first or second source of imports for Belize, Costa Rica, Honduras, Mexico, Nicaragua, Paraguay, Uruguay and Venezuela.

China, the second-largest contributor to UN budgets and peace-keeping operations in the world, has made remarkable progress in claiming leadership roles in major international organizations in recent years. In June 2019, China's Vice Minister of Agriculture Qu Dongyu was elected in the first ballot as director-general of the United Nations Food and Agriculture Organization (FAO), beating France's Catherine Geslain-Laneelle thanks to massive support from emerging countries. The stakes were high. The FAO had been run for a quarter-century by a representative of an emerging country. The FAO is an institution of major importance for a good portion of mankind. "This is a historic date, a new springboard" for agriculture and food in the world, the newly elected director-general commented, promising to do "everything to be impartial and neutral".

This diplomatic success was only the latest step in the strategy of clinching key positions in major international institutions that China has been carrying out for a decade. For example, in November 2018 Chinese communications and information technology (IT) engineer Zhao Houlin was re-elected for a second four-year term as the head of the International Telecommunication Union (ITU). In March 2015 China's Liu Fang was elected secretary-general of the International Civil Aviation Organization (ICAO). In June 2013 seasoned Chinese economic and financial manager Li Yong was appointed director-general of the United Nations Industrial Development Organization (UNIDO). A Chinese national appointed by UN Secretary-General Antonio Guterres also heads the UN Department of Economic and Social Affairs. Finally, China's Margaret Chan led the World Health Organization (WHO) between 2007 and 2017. China also had one of its nationals, Meng Hongwei, at the head of Interpol, the international organization that facilitates worldwide police cooperation, before he disappeared during a trip to China in September 2018. Meng later resurfaced during a corruption trial, where he pleaded guilty. He was sentenced in January 2020 to 13 and a half years in prison for corruption.

China has in recent years considerably strengthened its presence at the UN headquarters in New York, where it now has an efficient lobbying operation. "There are dozens of 'little hands' all over the UN premises, 'interns' without official status. We see them everywhere," a journalist working at the UN told me. At the UN Security Council, where it has been one of the five permanent members since 1971, China has exercised its veto power with relative parsimony, but it generally allies itself with Russia against the United States, the United Kingdom and France. China has also with increasing success blocked in UN bodies, in particular in the Human Rights Council in Geneva, Western attempts to adopt resolutions denouncing the human rights situation in China. Beijing even managed to have the Council adopt in July 2019 a resolution that it had itself submitted and which was largely favorable to China. This resolution stipulated, among other things, that "meeting the aspiration of the people for a better life is the priority of each State," and that efforts "to eradicate poverty... [are] of significant importance for the enjoyment of human rights." Meanwhile, Beijing overtook Washington in 2019 in the number of its embassies and consulates throughout the world, with a total of 276 diplomatic missions against 271 for the United States. (China now has, 2019) In peacekeeping operations, China has taken a place in the front row. Today, more than 2,500 Chinese soldiers are peace-keepers in Lebanon, Mali, the Democratic Republic of Congo and South Sudan.

China, which has more than 800 million internet users, has emerged in recent years as a master of cyberwarfare along with industrial espionage. Among computer attacks carried out in 2018 and 2019, four targeted Airbus subcontractors. Several security sources close to the case mentioned a group linked to the Chinese authorities, identified under the code name APT10. According to an industrial source working in cybersecurity, there is also a group of Chinese hackers that specializes in aerospace: the Jiangsu Province Ministry of State Security (JSSD), the regional branch of the Ministry of State Security (MSS) in the eastern region.[12] When queried, the Chinese Ministry of Foreign Affairs responded with a broad statement of principle. "I can tell you clearly that China is a staunch defender of cybersecurity and stands against all forms of cyberattacks," said ministry spokesman Geng Shuang. In February 2012 then US president Barack Obama received a 74-page report from Mandiant, an American company specializing in computer security. This report, the result of six years of investigation, revealed that hundreds of Chinese hackers were working on the internet under the guidance of People's Liberation Army (PLA) unit 61398. The unit's headquarters, according to the report, was a twelve-story Shanghai building that housed a cyber army under the close supervision and direction of the high command. The report dubbed the group "Advanced Persistent Threat 1". It alleged the unit had looted information from 141 American companies in 20 different sectors since 2010. China was also mobilizing significant resources, under the leadership of the PLA's 3rd department, to set up specialized internal security forces in cyberspace.

In 2015, Beijing created its equivalent of the US Cyber Command, named the Strategic Support Force, to bring together the PLA's resources in the cyber, space and electronic warfare fields. China has also been on the receiving end of cyberwarfare from the United States. According to the *Global Times*, the Chinese Communist Party's English-language daily, China was the main target of thousands of cyberattacks coming from IP addresses in the United States.

---

[12] Agence France-Presse, September 26, 2019.

Chinese experts quoted by the newspaper predicted that the Americans were preparing to wage a large-scale cyberwar, and stated that China is ready to launch a strong counterattack. "Aside from implanting viruses, the US has long been hacking information from the terminals of Chinese customers, and has been utilizing apps to tap, steal information and analyze the information they obtained," the Global Times quoted a Beijing-based military expert who also specializes in cybersecurity as saying. (Sun & Zhao, 2019)

The US military inaugurated in 2010 its Cyber Command which employs 6,000 experts and whose headquarters is located at Fort Meade in Maryland. But Washington also relies on many US defense firms active in the cyber protection and sabotage fields. In November 2018, at the meeting of the Internet Governance Forum (IGF) at UNESCO's headquarters, French President Emmanuel Macron launched the Paris Call for Trust and Security in Cyberspace. This statement calling for the development of common principles for securing cyberspace has so far attracted 564 supporters, including 67 governments, 358 private firms and 139 international organizations and civil society groups. China and the United States did not join it. Instead, the Chinese state controls information and censors the internet with its "Great Firewall". The Chinese leadership wants to both protect against external influences and internal risks (dissent, separatism) by filtering any information considered as harmful. The system works by self-regulation (censorship carried out by access providers), the use of an automated filtering system based on keywords and close monitoring by 50,000 agents who police the Web. It is the Ministry of Security State and its local offices that are responsible for enforcing the regulations, which are constantly being refined.

Beijing also claims its "indisputable" sovereignty over all the islands of the South China Sea, in particular the Spratlys and Paracels in Southeast Asia. Beijing delineates its claims by its controversial "nine-dashed line", a U-shaped line extending from the southern Chinese coast to the south of Malaysia, a huge area of some 3,500,000 square kilometers. China's claims were invalidated in 2016 by the Permanent Court of Arbitration (PCA) in The Hague at the request of the Philippines. Beijing has not given up. China proclaims its sovereignty over these islands and reefs based on historical considerations which are often fictitious. Beijing considers that the Spratly Islands and the Paracels have been Chinese territory for almost two millennia. China points to ancient manuscripts that speak of these islands as being Chinese, as well as pottery and coins found on them, as evidence. For Beijing, historical sources (the authenticity of which may be questioned) indicate that around 110 BC, the Han dynasty (206 BC–220 AD) installed an administration on the island of Hainan, to the south of the Chinese mainland, whose territory included the archipelagos of Nansha (Spratlys) and Xisha (Paracels). For experts, the existence of Han dynasty coins is not a convincing argument of Chinese control, but rather an indication of commercial relations between China and Southeast Asia. Some of these islands are also claimed by Vietnam, Taiwan, the Philippines, Malaysia and Brunei. This area has become a hotspot due mainly to its militarization by China. These other countries with claims on islands are competing for its fishery wealth and the probable presence of large undersea oil and natural gas deposits. In total, 10% of the world's fishing is carried out in the South China Sea. This area is also a strategic crossroads for trade routes of paramount importance as it is the shortest route between the North Pacific and the Indian Ocean. As a result of this strategy of occupation pursued since 1987, China now controls all of the Paracel Islands and a good part of the Spratlys. In June 2015, China claimed more than 1,200 hectares of land in the area, compared with 32 by Vietnam, 28 by Malaysia, five by the Philippines and three by Taiwan. Vietnam regularly protests against the incursion of Chinese ships into its exclusive economic zone (EEZ),[13] in vain. The Philippines and Indonesia are doing the same. But none of them have the military means to stand up to the crushing hold of China which will, in all probability, become even stronger in the years to come.

For the American scholar Graham Allison, today's China, like many ancient Chinese strategists, continues to think that "national greatness

---

[13] Maritime domain over which a coastal state exercises a sovereign right.

derives from sea power". (Allison, 2019 [2017]) China has, in recent years, significantly increased its presence in this area with the construction of artificial islands and military infrastructure on several islands, including runways that allow for the landing of combat aircraft and the deployment of missiles. China has amassed more than a thousand anti-ship missiles and a huge coastal fleet in the area. Dozens of submarines patrol these waters, armed with torpedoes and missiles able to sink enemy ships. In 2018 it installed electronic warfare equipment on two of its fortified outposts in the Spratlys (Fiery Cross and Mischief reefs). These powerful stations are capable of jamming communications and radar systems. In April 2018 China also deployed surface-to-sea and surface-to-air missiles on the Spratly reefs of Fiery Cross, Subi and Mischief, which are located to the east of Vietnam, west of the Philippines and very far south of mainland China. Allison says that by deploying "military capabilities that threaten US carriers and other capital ships, China has been steadily pushing the US Navy out of its adjacent seas". The scholar says anti-satellite weapons give China the capacity to jam or even destroy US intelligence, surveillance, and communication satellites over the area. "No longer does the United States have uncontested control of the sea and air along the thousand-mile wide corridor of ocean bordering China," he says. (*ibid.*)

In August 2019 the White House accused China of using "intimidation tactics" in the southern and eastern parts of the South China Sea. "The recent intensification of China's efforts to dissuade other countries in the South China Sea from exploiting its resources is worrying," tweeted John Bolton, then the White House's national security adviser. "The United States stands firmly with those who oppose coercive behavior and intimidation tactics that threaten regional peace and security," he added. The US 7th Fleet regularly sends warships through the Taiwan Strait in order to reinforce "freedom of navigation" rights.[14] France was doing so twice a year without any reaction from Beijing

---

[14] In addition to the United States and France, Australia, the United Kingdom, Japan and Canada regularly dispatch warships through the 160-kilometer-wide Taiwan Strait in order to demonstrate "freedom of navigation" rights.

until April 2019, when the *Vendémiaire* surveillance frigate crossed the Taiwan Strait. Chinese ships then carried out maneuvers described as "dangerous" by French authorities, while Beijing protested to Paris. In early September 2019, as if in response to China's increasing ambitions in the area, unprecedented naval maneuvers between the United States and ten Southeast Asian countries took place in the Gulf of Thailand with the participation of eight warships, four combat aircraft and more than a thousand soldiers. These exercises allowed their forces to "work together on shared maritime security priorities in the region," declared the Vice Admiral Phil Sawyer, commander of the US 7th Fleet.

In July 2020, Secretary of State Mike Pompeo unveiled a hardening of US policy towards Chinese territorial claims in the South China Sea. "We are making clear: Beijing's claims to offshore resources across most of the South China Sea are completely unlawful, as is its campaign of bullying to control them," he said in a statement. Pompeo evoked the 2016 ruling by the Permanent Court of Arbitration in The Hague which rejected Beijing's claims in the region. It was a considerable change in position by the United States, which had hitherto declined to take a position on the territorial disputes in the region and only affirmed "freedom of navigation" rights. The announcement followed Chinese military maneuvers at the beginning of the month around the Paracels that had abruptly raised tensions in the area known for its rich fishing grounds. Washington responded by sending to the area two aircraft carriers — the *Ronald Reagan* and the *Nimitz* — a deployment level not seen since 2014.

China also has a huge propaganda machine that is aimed not only at its citizens but at the outside world as well. The Chinese press is under the direct authority and control of the Party, just as the military, the judiciary and the educational system are. Journalists working for state media outlets, which constitute almost the entirety of the country's media landscape, have since the autumn of 2019 been required to take an exam to assess their loyalty to the authorities and the Party, as well as to test their knowledge about "Xi Jinping thought". A circular from the media supervisory board of the Chinese Communist Party's propaganda department broadcast in September 2019 announced that

10,000 journalists and editors working in fourteen media organizations in Beijing were to submit to a series of pilot tests in early October before the national exams. Throughout their careers, journalists are expected to report "positive news" about their country. Besides various magazines published in several languages,[15] Beijing maintains an elaborate system of radio and television channels broadcasting abroad. Its China Global Television Network (CGTN), a subsidiary of China Central Television (CCTV), has gained a foothold in London where it opened a regional hub in January 2018, after having set up such centers in Nairobi and Washington in 2012, to provide news on European business and politics "with a Chinese perspective". China Radio International (CRI) has the largest foreign service among Asian media, with more than fifty shortwave transmitters. CRI programs can be picked up on medium wave in most major cities along the eastern seaboard of the United States. The New China News Agency (Xinhua), founded in 1931 by the CCP, employs more than ten thousand people around the world and has offices in 140 countries. It is attached to the State Council and disseminates news that strictly adheres to the official Party line. The English-language *China Daily* is also responsible for expensive regular inserts extolling the glory of the regime and its President Xi Jinping, in about thirty world newspapers, including *The New York Times* and *Le Figaro*, which reach 13 million readers. China also exports its soft power[16] to Africa, in particular through editorial supplements in African newspapers and magazines.

Inside China, the press is under total control. The dissemination of foreign media is tightly restricted and closely censored. This is why

---

[15] One of the tools of Chinese propaganda intended for abroad is the monthly *China Today*, which available in Mandarin, English, Spanish, Arabic and German. On the cover of its September 2019 issue was emblazoned: "Human rights in China: Working for a happy life" and included on the subject articles entitled: "A Chinese way for the development of human rights" and "So that everyone enjoys extended human rights". Its society section included: "Tibet: Tourism and education bring a happy life and new vigor and vitality in Xinjiang".

[16] Soft power, as formulated in 1990 by Harvard professor Joseph Nye is "when one country gets other countries to want what it wants".

Google, Instagram, Facebook, Twitter, and Snapchat have been blocked for years by China's "Great Firewall". The same goes for the websites of *The New York Times*, BBC, *The Guardian*, *The Washington Post*, Reuters, AFP, *El País*, *The Hindu*, *Der Spiegel*, *The Economist*, *Le Monde*, *Liberation*, Radio France International and others. In Beijing, foreign correspondents are subject to surveillance at all times, especially those who are fluent in Chinese. Those who break the unwritten rules imposed by the censors are either expelled or their residence visas are not renewed. Journalists guilty of "malicious attacks" against China "are not welcome", the government said in August 2019 as it effectively ejected from the country a *Wall Street Journal* reporter who co-wrote an article that said Ming Chai, one of the cousins of President Xi Jinping, had been caught up in a money-laundering investigation opened by Australian authorities. Chun Han Wong, a Singaporean citizen who had been working in the Beijing bureau of the American daily since 2014, did not have his press credentials renewed when they expired, meaning he could no longer work in the country.

China has also had another powerful soft power instrument since 2004 in the form of a vast network of Confucius Institutes.[17] These non-profit cultural establishments, which are inspired by the networks of Alliances Française and the British Council, promote Chinese culture and offer language instruction from teachers recruited and paid for by Beijing. There were 548 of these institutes across the world in 2019, including 14 in France, and they have dispensed some 12,000 hours of lessons per year. In addition, some 1,193 "Confucius classes" were held in primary and secondary schools. China is betting that thanks to these institutes, foreign nationals will become more interested in Chinese culture and be more receptive to the emergence of China on the international scene. For critics, these institutes are actually a tool for relaying

---

[17] The director of the Confucius Institute in Brussels, Song Xinning, was denied a residence permit by Belgium in October 2019, thus effectively banning him from staying in the 26 countries of the Schengen zone for eight years, for allegedly working with Chinese intelligence in Belgium, an allegation that Song denied.

Chinese propaganda and reassuring images of a peaceful and developed China.[18]

The advance of Chinese soft power remains limited in scope, however. For Michel Jean:

> Having become a fan of soft power, the Chinese leadership is now trying to make the "Chinese model" enviable, boasting about its past and national culture. It draws upon its history for justifications for land claims, propagates myths of Chinese exceptionalism, of its peaceful traditions and non-expansionism, all the while prohibiting the evocation of the darkest pages of the empire as well as those of the Communist regime. (Jan, 2014)

Western observers of China generally agree that the "Chinese model" is not really exportable. Moreover, Beijing has not been doing a very good job of promoting it lately. Its policies against the Uighurs in Xinjiang, the Tibetans and Hong Kong have seriously and sustainably damaged China's image.[19] As has China's response to the coronavirus pandemic. A recent survey of 14 advanced nations by the US-based Pew Research Center found that unfavorable views of

---

[18] The American government has regularly expressed its concern about Confucius Institutes. The US Senate Committee on Homeland Security and Governmental Affairs (HSGAC) warned in 2019 about the lack of transparency of these institutes and their role in the dissemination of Chinese propaganda on American soil. The same year, several American universities decided to sever their ties with Confucius Institutes which then had to close their doors (Kang & Ottone, 2019).

[19] According to credible studies, at least one million Uighur, Kazakh and Kyrgyz Muslims are currently being held in "reeducation camps" in Xinjiang, making this autonomous region in northwestern China the largest twenty-first-century detention camp in the world. China speaks of "vocational training centers". US Secretary of State Mike Pompeo called China's treatment of the Uighurs the "stain of the century". China has also been accused of large-scale organ removal from Uighur detainees and members of the Falun Gong sect for transplants on Western patients, making this appalling practice a lucrative business that sources say earns Beijing more than $1 billion per year. Uighur intellectual Ilham Tohti, who is serving a life sentence in China for separatism, received on October 24, 2019 the Sakharov Prize for Human Rights awarded by the European Parliament.

China have reached historic highs. "In most countries, views soured significantly since just last year," it found, noting that the shift "comes amid widespread criticism over how China has handled the coronavirus pandemic." That being said, respondents still gave China better marks than the United States for the way it handled the pandemic, and Xi Jinping similarly bested Donald Trump. "While these changes since last year are stark, in some countries, they are part of a larger trajectory," the researchers who carried out the survey noted. Unfavorable opinions of China have been growing in some nations for several years. And while younger people still tended to have a better opinion of China than older people did, the survey found that for the first time a majority of young Australians and Americans hold unfavorable views of China. (Pew Research Center, 2020)

Chapter 4

A Battleground for Two Titans: The Race for High-Tech Supremacy

ill the United States lose its dominant position as the world's laboratory for the advanced technologies of tomorrow? Beijing has committed colossal sums to become the undeniable global champion of the technological fields that will shape the future. And what about artificial intelligence, the new instrument of a system of social coercion, as well as robotics, a field that may define the direction of human development for the coming decades?

> "Many small people, in small places, doing small things, can change the world."
>
> Eduardo Galeano (1940–2015)
> Uruguayan journalist, writer and novelist

China has publicly declared its determination to become a technological superpower. The world already owes China for "four great inventions" (the printing press, gunpowder, the compass and paper). Today it intends to regain its status as a great nation for innovation. With the "Made in China 2025" plan unveiled by the State Council in 2015, it wants to play a key role in ten sectors considered to be crucial for the future: IT, robotics, aerospace, advanced naval and railway industries, zero-emission vehicles, energy, agricultural equipment, new materials and bio-medicine. Over the ten years from 2008 to 2017, Chinese spending on research and development (R&D) increased by 900% and reached $400 billion in 2020. "It's dizzying!" says Antoine Mynard, director of the Beijing office of France's National Scientific Research Center (CNRS). (Robert, 2018) "Nothing can apparently prevent China from being the Number One in the world in all areas, including technology, in the next ten to fifteen years. The Americans obviously cannot accept that and will do everything to prevent it. And China is also preparing for it. The whole world system is reorganizing itself around that," said France's former foreign minister, Hubert Védrine, at the launch of the latest edition of the *Atlas des crises et des conflits* (*Atlas of Crises and Conflicts*) at the French Institute for International and Strategic Affairs (IRIS) in September 2019. (Boniface & Védrine, 2019) Today, there are more than 800 million Chinese internet users, the vast majority of whom own smartphones which now number 1.3 billion units, or three times more than in America. In 2017, Chinese consumers spent $8 trillion, or fifty times more than Americans. After being dependent on foreign technology for its development, China today is seeking to become autonomous and to be at the heart of the next industrial revolution. Over the past decade, it has become the world's number two in terms of R&D investments behind the United States and ahead of Japan. Its objective is to devote 2.5% of its GDP to research in 2020 against 2.05% in 2016. Why the push? Because "we can't always furnish our tomorrows with what others produced yesterday. We cannot afford to fall behind in this crucial race. We must catch up and try to overtake the others," said President Xi Jinping. Chinese companies heard the message loud and clear, as illustrated by the 2018–2019 ranking of the world's 100 most innovative firms compiled by Derwent and Clarivate Analytics. In 2016, there were still no Chinese companies listed. Huawei made the list in 2017, and the car manufacturer BYD and smartphone maker Xiaomi made their debut in 2018. But is a country that gags individual freedoms a place where innovation can really take place? "A country without political freedoms could not truly innovate, and people without freedom of expression couldn't create a thriving cultural industry. It's a mantra woven deep into our American psyche," points out Matt Sheehan. (Sheehan, 2019) Reality today seems to prove the opposite.

The cradle of the US high-tech industry is the famous Silicon Valley, which stretches forty kilometers southeast from San Francisco, between San Mateo and Fremont. Some 2.6 million people live there and 39% of them are between the ages of 20 and 44. The average annual income is $75,000. Some 11,500 high-tech companies operate there, employing 420,000 people and generating $275 billion in annual sales or equivalent to the size of Finland's economy. If Silicon Valley was an independent territory, it would be the 12th largest economy in the world. More than 15% of patents filed in the United States are by companies, universities or laboratories located in Silicon Valley. The area also has close ties to the military and security industries. This is where the transistor was born in 1947, the integrated circuit in 1961, the microprocessor in 1971, Apple's first personal computer in 1976, and then the first web portal in 1995. This is also where many high-tech companies are headquartered, notes Laurent Carroué, research director at the French Institute of Geopolitics. (Carroué, 2019) "The economic development of the GAFAM and other Silicon Valley businesses was facilitated by the absence of initial competition in technologies whose emergence had been strongly supported by the defense sector," says Christian Harbulot, director at the Economic Warfare School of Paris. "'Invisible' links with a power policy are reinforced by an implicit strategy to conquer the digital world that has been adopted by the new American elites," he adds. (Harbulot, 2017: 94–95) China's answer to Silicon Valley is Zhongguancun, located in the Haidian district northwest of Beijing. This high-tech hub, which extends over 488 square kilometers, brings together 41 research institutes of the Chinese Academy of Sciences as well as a dozen universities, including Beijing University, Tsinghua, Beijing University of Technology, and more than 210 research institutes and various laboratories. Each year more than 100,000 students graduate from these institutions. In 2019, there were more than 19,000 companies dedicated to developing new technologies operating in Zhongguancun's technology parks, including the flagships of the internet and computer industries such as Sina Corp.,

Baidu and Lenovo.[1] Almost half of Chinese "unicorns" have set up shop there.[2] Some 80 start-ups are founded daily. Already in 2009 this great Chinese business incubator surpassed Silicon Valley in the number of high-tech IPOs, and this is expected to continue for the foreseeable future. The government has also started construction on a 55-hectare technology park in the Mentougou district, 60 kilometers west of Beijing, at a cost of $2.1 billion. This park, whose opening is slated for 2024, will be entirely dedicated to research on artificial intelligence.

US internet firms generated $2.1 trillion of revenue in 2018, or 10% of the country's total GDP[3], an indication of the meteoric rise in importance of this sector in the daily life of Americans. The internet is an American invention. The first computer network was established on November 21, 1969, between the University of California at Los Angeles and the Stanford Research Institute. From December 5 of the same year, by adding a link between the University of Utah and the University of California at Santa Barbara, a network with four nodes was born. American giants Intel and AMD (Advanced Micro Devices) remain the undisputed world leaders in semiconductors and microprocessors, areas in which US industry retains a significant technological lead. Computers from Chinese colossus Lenovo for international markets are all equipped with US processors. Founded in July 1968 by Gordon Moore, Robert Noyce and Andrew Grove, Intel Corporation is the world's leading semiconductor manufacturer by revenue. AMD, based in the Silicon Valley town of Santa Clara, was founded in May 1969 by a group of engineers and executives of Fairchild Semiconductor. Processors from these two manufacturers dominate the global market for personal computers. But China intends to catch up soon. In 2019

---

[1] Lenovo became the world's top manufacturer of personal computers in 2013, with revenue hitting $51 billion in its 2018–2019 reporting year. It bought IBM's PC business in 2005.

[2] China has passed the United States in the number of "unicorns" with 206 in June 2019 compared to 203 in the United States, out of a world total of 494 (Hurun Research Institute, 2019b).

[3] Reuters, September 26, 2019.

it produced 16% of the world's semiconductors and it aims to hit 40% in 2020 and 70% in 2025. In May 2018, Xi Jinping met with key researchers and engineers to encourage them to work to achieve technological independence for China in this area. In October of the same year, the Chinese government created a fund endowed with $29 billion earmarked for the development of the national semiconductor industry. "The question is not whether China has the engineers to manufacture semiconductors. It's whether they can make competitive products," says Piero Scaruffi, a Silicon Valley researcher specializing in artificial intelligence. (Vincent, 2019) At the beginning of December 2019, the Communist Party ordered all Chinese authorities to stop using "foreign" software and computers by the end of 2022. This directive specifically targets American products. Some 20 to 30 million computers are concerned and should be replaced by products made by Lenovo or other Chinese manufacturers.

The United States and China are leaders in artificial intelligence (the ensemble of techniques that allow machines to mimic the cognitive processes of human beings; commonly referred to as AI), a key area that may revolutionize the future. According to PricewaterhouseCoopers (PwC, an international network of companies specializing in auditing, accounting and consulting), the development of AI will translate into an increase in global GDP by $15.7 trillion by 2030. Almost $7 trillion of this wealth will accrue to China. Half of global AI investments in 2019 were carried out by firms in three Chinese cities: Beijing, Shanghai and Guangzhou. In August 2018, at the first World Artificial Intelligence Conference held in Melbourne, "a third of the presentations were made by Chinese laboratories", observes Bertrand Braunschweig, director of the Inria-Saclay research center.

Until recently, the United States was the undisputed leader in AI research. Things have changed, and China has now taken the lead in this rapidly developing field. "The Chinese government unveiled its AI development plan in July 2017," says Charles Thibout, a researcher at the French Institute for International and Strategic Affairs and an AI specialist. "Initially, the annual budget was $20 billion and forecast to rise to $60 billion in 2025. But these figures may have already been surpassed. According to the Pentagon, China's annual budget may have already reached $70 billion. That's much more than the $4 billion annually in public money that the United States — historically the great power of AI — has been spending in this area." But in the United States it has been private firms that have taken the lead in investing in this field: "Last year, the GAFAM spent between 40 and 60 billion dollars on research and development in AI," Thibout adds. (Tellier, 2019) Today, the BATX (the giants of the Chinese Web: Baidu, Alibaba, Tencent and Xiaomi) are positioning themselves as competitors to their American rivals. One of their AI experts is Kai-Fu Lee. A researcher born in Taiwan and who works in Beijing, Lee formerly served as president of Google China and his book *AI Superpowers, China, Silicon Valley and the New World Order*, has become a global bestseller. (Lee K.L., 2019) In an interview, he explains:

> Today, we have two countries that are the driving forces in this AI revolution: the United States and China [...] In China, the competition is really tough, and the entrepreneurs are working crazy hours. There is a cultural component, because it's the first generation that has this opportunity, while their parents were poor. When this historical phenomenon happens, the work ethic is very strong and people don't burn out. Finally, the Chinese government and local authorities strongly support the AI sector. (Mahler, 2019)

Lee predicts that within fifteen years, 40–50% of today's jobs will no longer exist in the United States, in particular research assistants, translators, accountants, truck drivers, divers, hematologists and agricultural workers. "Whoever becomes the leader in the field of artificial intelligence will be the master of the world," declared Russian President Vladimir Putin in September 2017 during a meeting with young Russians. (Tanguy, 2017)

One widely used AI application in China is facial recognition. After a staggering boom that saw the deployment of millions of surveillance cameras throughout the main cities, the AI-enabled system already allows authorities to identify those who commit crimes on the street and track and detain fugitives. But the facial recognition algorithm paired with more than 200 million surveillance cameras also allows the authorities to crack down on even the smallest incivility, thus intruding into the private life of citizens. It is impossible not to recall the frightening world of Big Brother that George Orwell created in his dystopian masterpiece *1984*.[4] (Orwell, 1949) The roll out across China of the "social credit" system which assigns "good" and "bad" points for certain behavior to "good" and "bad" citizens via a system that includes the surveillance and facial recognition network was planned for 2020. Smoking in a public space, being rude, not paying bills or taxes, use of an expired train ticket: such infractions may result in punishments including a ban on using trains or planes, being prevented from taking out a bank loan or even buying an apartment. (Bougon, 2019) On the other hand, reporting a criminal earns one points. According to a report from the Chinese National Credit Information Center, China blocked 17.5 million "discredited" citizens from buying plane tickets and another 5.5 million from buying train tickets in 2018. (Cohen, 2019) Cameras are now being deployed in Chinese schools and universities to track the attendance and behavior of students. Playing with a smartphone during class is now very hard to get away with. Since December 2019, following a directive of the Ministry of Industry and Information Technology, Chinese citizens who wish to obtain a SIM card for their smartphones must allow themselves to be scanned by the facial recognition system, in order to "protect the rights and interests of citizens in cyberspace". At the end of September 2019, Chinese engineers unveiled a very high definition camera that is capable of identifying all the spectators in a stadium. Meanwhile, there has been increasing resistance to mass surveillance in Western countries. In January 2020, the European Commission briefly considered the adoption of a

---

[4] It should be noted that in Western countries people are subjected to continuous digital surveillance. The latest tools allow knowing almost all of the lifestyle habits of connected populations, thanks to the monitoring of their activities on smartphones and personal computers, including their email. In 2013, revelations about the surveillance capabilities of the US security agency NSA, caused a sensation and exposed the extent of the surveillance and the lack of privacy of citizens. France, for its part, in November 2019 became the first European country to introduce facial recognition to identify oneself for conducting administrative services online, a system called Alicem.

moratorium on using facial recognition technology in public places for a period of five years. Many US cities including San Francisco; Somerville, Massachusetts; and Oakland, California have banned the use of this controversial technology. But China is going even further. It has extended DNA testing across the entire population, from birth, having experimented with this unprecedented measure on the Uighur people in Xinjiang.

In August 2019, the European Chamber of Commerce in China raised a cry of alarm that the "social credit" system now also targets businesses. It warned in a report that it is not "inconceivable that the Corporate SCS could mean life or death for individual companies." (Berger, 2019) According to the organization, it is high time for European businesses to realize how the similar but separate social credit system for businesses that Chinese authorities are implementing will impact their operations. In mid-September, the *South China Morning Post* announced that Chinese authorities had carried out an evaluation of more than 33 million national businesses. Beijing hopes to build by 2021 a single database for rating companies. Facial recognition technology is already used in a number of stores. It is no longer necessary for shoppers to pull out a credit card or their smartphone to pay for purchases. Just stand in front of a camera that will quickly identify you and then debit your bank account. "No more need to take your phone with you. You can go out shopping without taking anything," says Bo Hu, the IT director of Wedome. (*En Chine*, 2019) This popular bakery chain which offers Western breads and pastries adapted to Chinese tastes already uses facial recognition terminals at hundreds of points of sale. Despite the use of AI for the Autopilot self-driving system in his Tesla electric cars, US entrepreneur Elon Musk remains cautious about the technology. At the 2nd annual AI conference held in Shanghai on August 29, 2019, where he faced off against Jack Ma, the former boss of Alibaba[5], Musk noted that computers were becoming so fast they

---

[5] Jack Ma is China's richest man with a fortune estimated at $40 billion. Alibaba, the Chinese e-commerce giant that employs 86,000 people, had $56 billion in revenue during its 2018–2019 fiscal year and is expected to reach $70 billion in 2019–2020.

were likely to find humans slow. "Human speech to a computer will sound like very slow tonal wheezing, kind of like whale sounds," he said. "So, the computer will just get impatient if nothing else. It'll be like talking to a tree — that's humans." Musk also worried that machines could eventually turn against humans. (Samama, 2019) Jack Ma parried calmly that machines don't have real wisdom. "Computers only have chips, men have the heart. It's the heart where the wisdom comes from." Meanwhile, Microsoft chief Satya Nadella dropped his normal reserve on October 6, 2019, to condemn US sanctions against China, in particular in the field of AI:

> "A lot of AI research happens in the open, and the world benefits from knowledge being open… That to me is what's been true since the Renaissance and the scientific revolution. Therefore, I think, for us to say that we will put barriers on it may in fact hurt more than improve the situation everywhere."[6] (Lee D., 2019)

The United States, on the other hand, remains the leader in the field of supercomputers. America created the first computer. The ENIAC (Electronic Numerical Integrator And Computer) was born in 1945 at the University of Pennsylvania. It weighed 30 tons and had computational power comparable to that of a small modern calculator. In October 2019, Google announced it had passed a major technological milestone using a quantum supercomputer that succeeded in performing a calculation in 3 minutes and 20 seconds that would have taken ten thousand years for the largest conventional supercomputers. America already had a significant lead over China with the Summit supercomputer located in the Oak Ridge National Laboratory in Tennessee, the most powerful in the world with a calculation speed of

---

See Duncan Clark, Alibaba, the incredible story of Jack Ma, the Chinese billionaire (2017).
[6]It should be noted that Microsoft's R&D activities in China are more important than those carried out in the rest of the world outside of the United States. Microsoft founder Bill Gates inaugurated Microsoft's first office in China in 1992. The company currently employs more than 200 researchers on its premises in Beijing.

143.5 petaflops (a petaflop is a million billion floating-point operations per second). By comparison, the fastest Chinese supercomputer, the Sunway TaihuLight, reaches only 93 petaflops.

On a different note, in October 2019 Xi Jinping officially lent his support to accelerating the development in China of the new technology called *blockchain*.[7] The Chinese president, who was speaking while presiding over a group study session of the Politburo of the ruling Chinese Communist Party on the development of this technology, added that China was to become a "world leader" in the field. "There is a need to strengthen basic research, value innovation and ensure that China takes the lead in the emerging *blockchain* technology, in order to occupy a dominant position in innovation and to reap the new industrial benefits," he said. (Mable, 2019) *Blockchain* is still in an early stage of development. It may be thought of as a database that contains the history of all exchanges made between its users since its creation. This database is distributed — it is shared by its different users without an intermediary. It is secure — everyone can monitor operations. Cryptocurrencies are a derivative application of the technology. Transactions between users of the network are grouped by blocks. Each block is validated by nodes of the network called "miners", using techniques that vary by *blockchain*. The Bitcoin *blockchain* uses a so-called proof-of-work technique that consists of solving complex algorithmic problems to be selected to validate transactions. The potential fields of exploitation are huge: banking, insurance, pharmaceuticals, supply chain management, the agri-food industry, international trade, retail distribution, aeronautics, automotive. *Blockchain* technology is already being widely implemented in China, in sectors such as digital finance, the Internet of Things, smart manufacturing, supply chain management and e-commerce. The authorities of the southern city of Guangzhou lost no time in reacting to Xi Jinping's call by announcing the creation of an investment fund endowed with one billion yuan ($142 million) for the development of this new technology, hoping

---

[7] Blockchain is a technology for storing and distributing information without central control.

that other cities will follow suit. Finally, China announced during the winter of 2019–2020 its intention to soon introduce a cryptocurrency, becoming the first state to do so.

A high-tech sector in which China leads along with Japan is robotics. China alone accounted for 36% of the world's production of robots in 2017 (138,000 units), more than the total manufactured in the United States and Europe. Japan remains the world champion with a market share of 56%. China lags behind in terms of the number of robots deployed per worker, however. Elsewhere in Asia, the adoption of robots has been particularly dynamic. South Korea, where 710 industrial robots are deployed for every 10,000 employees, is the worldwide champion, followed by Singapore at 658. China finds itself far behind with just 97 robots per 10,000 workers, despite the extraordinary number of robots being deployed in certain companies present in the country, like Foxconn.[8] But such a classification should be put into perspective. As China boasts the world's largest labor force, the robot to human ratio is naturally lower. The United States comes in at 200, positioning it in the middle. In Europe, Germany leads with 309 units. France has just 137 but remains above the global average of 85 industrial robots per 10,000 workers. Worldwide robot sales more than doubled between 2013 and 2017 (+114%) and should continue to climb by 14% per year through the 2018–2021 period. China, Japan, South Korea, the United States and Germany together represented 73% of robot sales in 2017. By the end of 2020, some 950,000 of the three million industrial robots operating worldwide (a three-fold increase on 2007) will be in China.[9]

Since the end of 2010 Xi Jinping has also been nursing along another gigantic plan: the birth of the Greater Bay Area (GBA), which is located in the Pearl River Delta in the south of China. This program, covering an area of 60,000 square kilometers, plans to connect nine

---

[8] Foxconn is China's largest private employer with around one million employees, including a large number of temporary workers. The Taiwanese company's factories on the Chinese mainland assemble many phones, notably iPhones on behalf of Apple.
[9] International Federation of Robotics, October 18, 2018.

cities in the province of Guangdong: Guangzhou, Shenzhen, Zhuhai, Foshan, Zhongshan, Dongguan, Huizhou, Jiangmen, Zhaoqing and of course Hong Kong and Macao. The region's population totals 80 million, including 7.5 million in the city of Hong Kong alone. This new region intends to compete with not only the San Francisco bay area that includes Silicon Valley, but also the Tokyo and New York metropolitan areas. Within the GBA, there is considerable industrial specialization between the cities. Shenzhen holds a dominant position in the mobile telephony sector (Huawei has its headquarters there) and consumer electronics, while Foshan specializes in household goods (coffee machines, rice cookers, refrigerators). For Dongguan, it is sporting goods, while Zhuhai does a bit of everything. Annual GDP per capita for GBA residents is 20,000 euros ($23,700). Chinese authorities aim to drive this up to 50,000 euros ($59,280) by 2030 — the equivalent of Germany!

Shenzhen, which is at the heart of this new rapid development zone, was just 40 years ago a small, quiet and unremarkable fishing village of a few thousand souls. The start signal for the great upheaval was Shenzhen's designation in 1980 as a Special Economic Zone (SEZ) as part of Deng Xiaoping's new policy of economic reform and openness. All four zones that were created were located in the southern provinces of Guangdong and Fujian. Since then Shenzhen has experienced breathtaking development and become Chinese capitalism's main center for experimentation. The city of 12.5 million residents which neighbors Hong Kong has become the cradle of China's biotechnology, internet, new energy, IT and environmental protection industries. All taxis, buses and scooters are electric in Shenzhen. Three million companies, large and small, have set up shop there, including 5,000 so-called IT solution providers which employ 150,000 engineers, and 4,000 industrial design studios.[10] "In the 1970s, we stopped there while taking the train from Guangzhou to Hong Kong. It was just a very

---

[10] David Li, director of the Shenzhen Open Innovation Lab, founder of the first Chinese hackerspace, speaking at the Abundance 360 Summit, in Beverly Hills, California, on February 18, 2019.

small village surrounded by rice fields then," Michel Jan recalls.[11] For David Li, director of Shenzhen Open Innovation Lab, the city has assumed a central role in China's economy:

> Shenzhen's opening made it the first Special Economic Zone in China. The city has become the largest laboratory for China's new economic system. In forty years, Shenzhen has become China's third city by GDP. It accounts for 90% of the production of home electronics and for 70% of the total production of mobile phones in the country. Starting from nothing, the city of Shenzhen has grown into a unique technological center in China. Shenzhen spends more of its GDP on R&D than Shanghai, Beijing or Guangzhou. This phenomenon has already been visible for a decade. The Transsion company has just successfully entered the stock market. This company now exports around 100 million mobile phones per year. It alone represents 35% of the African mobile market yet hardly anyone outside the continent has ever heard of it. Today, Chinese and American high-tech companies are too closely linked to one another to be able to imagine separating them. Just think that 80% of the mobile phone components sold by the American giant Qualcomm[12] are manufactured in China. Some 99.9% of Apple's mobile phones are assembled in China. The United States occupies a dominant position in semiconductors and microprocessors. China is stronger in industrial applications.[13]

When you arrive in Shenzhen, you are greeted by large signs telling you to "Realize your dreams" and that it is "The city of the future". No need to apply for a visa at the Chinese consulate. Shenzhen is a city open to the world. Coming from Hong Kong, you can obtain a special visa for Shenzhen in less than an hour. In the city, when night falls, the skyscrapers of the financial district are lit up with a thousand lights. The Eiffel Tower can't compete. In early October 2019, I took advantage of a stay in Hong Kong to walk the streets of Shenzhen, where major thoroughfares and squares are under the watchful eye of surveillance cameras. I had never before set foot in Shenzhen. I wandered the alleys

---

[11] Interview with the author, October 16, 2019.
[12] With sales of $25.3 billion in 2018, Qualcomm is a leading company in providing technology and components for mobile phones.
[13] Interview with the author, September 30, 2019.

of the Dafen painters' quarter and, to my amazement, I discovered an oasis of calm in this ultramodern megalopolis. In the painting workshops, I found portraits of Deng Xiaoping, the city's benefactor, as well as of Xi Jinping. But I also saw portraits of Jack Ma, China's symbol of entrepreneurial and social success, and even more surprisingly, of Bill Gates!

The Greater Bay Area initiative has seven axes: creating an international innovation and technology "hub"; accelerating infrastructure connectivity; building a "globally competitive" industrial system; implementing a "forward-looking" ecological conservation plan; adopting a comprehensive approach to improving quality of life at home, work and while commuting; cooperating with the Belt and Road Initiative (BRI) program; and finally, deepening cooperation between Guangdong province, Hong Kong and Macao. This region is already bringing online giant state-of-the-art infrastructure projects, which attest to its extraordinary dynamism. Take for example the $10.8 billion high-speed train link between the cities of Guangzhou and Hong Kong inaugurated in September 2018 that allows travelers to cover the 100 kilometers between the two cities in forty-eight minutes, compared with two hours previously. It links up to the Guangzhou-Beijing line, the longest high-speed train line in the world which cut the travel time on the 2,298-kilometer journey from 24 to eight hours when it opened in December 2012. Another gigantic work of art is the huge bridge connecting Hong Kong to the former Portuguese colony of Macao via Zhuhai. The longest sea bridge in the world was inaugurated in October 2018. This architectural masterpiece faced massive technological challenges to span 55 kilometers and required $22 billion and nine years of work to complete. It was finished just a month after the Guangzhou-Hong Kong high-speed rail line. It now connects all the megacities of the Pearl River estuary by a motorway above the sea.

Civil aviation is another sector in which China is about to close its technological gap. Aircraft manufactured by Airbus, Boeing and ATR currently reign supreme in this sector which had enjoyed very strong growth and is still seen as set for further expansion in the decades to come despite the COVID-19 pandemic. But Beijing is grooming competitors, including its first medium-haul commercial aircraft, the Comac C919, the largest ever designed and built by China. Announced in 2010 for 2014, the inaugural flight took place on May 5, 2017. The first deliveries are expected by 2022, four years behind schedule. Certification for the narrow-body airliner, originally planned for 2020, is likely to be postponed to 2021. The aircraft aims to compete head-on with the Airbus A320 and Boeing 737 families of aircraft. Designed by the Commercial Aircraft Corporation of China (Comac), it will be able to transport 158 passengers up to 4,075 km in a standard configuration, and up to 174 in a high-density configuration and up to 5,555 km in a long-range version. At the end of 2018, the C919 had registered 815 firm orders, options and purchase commitments from 28 customers, mainly from Chinese aircraft leasing firms but also airlines such as Air China, China Eastern Airlines, China Southern Airlines and Hainan Airlines. (Ricci, 2019)

But concerns are growing over China's access to key American-made components for the C919. The C919 relies on imports of a number of crucial parts, from its engines to its flight-control systems, so access to US suppliers such as General Electric (GE), Honeywell International and Rockwell Collins is vital for future deliveries of the new model. The C919 will initially be powered by CFM LEAP-1C engines (CFM is the joint venture between the American company General Electric and France's Safran that manufacturers engines for the latest versions of the A320 and Boeing 737), although the Chinese aeronautical industry intends to soon develop its own engines.

One gets an impression of great cleanliness when visiting the Comac[14] assembly plant, in the Pudong industrial zone in Shanghai. During a visit there, a plane carrying the number 6 sat in the middle of the huge hall which measures over 600 meters long by 150 wide. This aircraft was the last prototype before serial production. A giant Chinese flag measuring 20 meters by 10 overlooked the hall and 20 young engineers and technicians were hard at work on a Saturday.

---

[14]Visit on October 26, 2019.

Visitors were shepherded for their tour along a raised footbridge. It was forbidden to take photos. The visit lasts at most ten minutes. Thirty percent of the aircraft built in this factory are destined for the Chinese market. The rest will be exported. The development of the aircraft has cost some $10 Billion, an amount comparable to what Boeing spent on the 737 and Airbus on the A320. Comac called on its best aerospace engineers for the aircraft's development, as well as about 200 Western consultants, including several veterans of Airbus and Boeing.[15] The C919 program makes extensive use of the best American and European subcontractors. The wiring of the aircraft was thus entrusted to Safran (50,000 cables per aircraft).[16] For these Western companies, the choice was to refuse to cooperate with Comac or agree to sign contracts, knowing that the Chinese would one day attain their goals anyway. Companies like Safran invest enormously in R&D in the hope of keeping their technological edge, and ahead of competitors and those who would copy their designs. The C919 is mostly constructed of metal and not composite materials. Comac plans to produce 50 aircraft per year during the first phase. In addition, Comac and the Russian United Aircraft Corp. (UAC) are developing together a long-haul airliner, the wide-body C929. A future competitor of the Airbus A350 and Boeing 787, the aircraft with a range of 12,000 kilometers and a capacity for 260 passengers should make its first flight in 2023 before entering service two years later. The Chinese aerospace industry is also manufacturing its first commercial regional transport aircraft, the MA700, which is being assembled in the factories of the Xi'an Aircraft Industrial Corporation. The turboprop aircraft with a range of 2,700 km and the capacity to carry 78 passengers bears a striking resemblance to the Franco-Italian ATR 72-600 with which it will become a direct competitor. The first test flight was scheduled for late 2020 and the plane is expected to arrive on the market by 2022.

China will then have a complete range of civil aircraft that are as efficient as their Western competitors but much cheaper.

---

[15] According to a French source in the industry.
[16] Via the Saifei joint venture in which Comac has a 51% stake and Safran 49%.

The manufacturing costs of the C919 should be half that of Boeing 737s and Airbus A320s. The aerospace sector is one of ten targeted under the "Made in China 2025" plan. Before the COVID-19 pandemic struck, China was expected to become the world's leading commercial aviation market between 2022 and 2024. There will thus be room for these Chinese planes in the future, especially considering that between new orders and the renewal of the existing global fleet, some 35,000 to 40,000 planes will be needed over the next 20 years. Approximately 42% of that demand will come from Asia. In 2018, airlines carried 4.3 billion passengers, a record figure. China alone will need to buy 8,090 new aircraft by 2038, an outlay of some $3 trillion, according to forecasts by Boeing. Within a decade, it expects one in five commercial aircraft in the world will be Chinese. (Reid, 2019) While those estimates were pre-pandemic, and the aviation sector has been hit hard, it will likely only delay growth by a few years. One figure that shows this growth potential is the fact that currently the average person in China takes just 0.43 trips per year, against 2.70 in the United States.

One can, of course, question the incredible speed with which China has perfected sophisticated planes, given that it took the United States and Europe several decades to develop them. The question has been raised whether China resorted to industrial espionage to speed along its efforts in the sector. According to an investigation by CrowdStrike, a firm that specializes in the protection of companies against cyberattacks, the development of the C919 aircraft may have been aided by cyberespionage carried out by Chinese companies linked to the Ministry of State Security against several Western aerospace companies during the period between 2010 and 2015. China has flatly denied such accusations of industrial espionage. (Crowdstrike, 2019)

China has also pushed forward with the infrastructure needed for a larger civil aviation industry to operate. In September 2019 it inaugurated Beijing Daxing airport, the largest in the world. With four airstrips and 268 parking spaces for aircraft, Beijing Daxing will be able to handle 72 million passengers per year when it reaches full capacity in 2025, and there are plans to expand capacity to 100 million passengers per year in 2040. The airport was designed by ADP Ingenierie, a subsidiary of Paris Airports (ADP), in partnership with the Anglo-Iraqi firm Zaha Hadid Architects. Its one-piece roof spans an area equivalent to 25 football fields. A metro and high-speed rail station are located directly under the terminal. An express line should make it possible to reach the city center in about 20 minutes. (*Chine: le nouvel aéroport*, 2019) Forty thousand workers were employed on the project which cost 120 billion yuan ($17 billion). Including rail and road connections, the total bill rises to 400 billion yuan ($61 billion). I remember arriving at Beijing's military and civil airport in 1980 during my first trip to the Chinese capital. It resembled a tiny provincial aerodrome. The new Daxing airport is yet another manifestation of China's fascination with gigantism.

Finally, in the last element of China's conquest of air and space, it will soon have a wide range of launchers for commercial satellites. The China Rocket Co., a subsidiary of the state-owned China Aerospace Science and Technology Corporation, was due to launch in 2020 its new Smart Dragon 2 rocket capable of putting 500 kg into orbit at an altitude of 500 km. The Smart Dragon 3, scheduled to go up in 2021, will be able to lift 1.5 tons into a similar orbit.[17] Alongside its Long March launchers, these rockets will give China a wide range of commercial lift capability to compete with American and Russian launchers as well as Europe's Ariane 5 rocket (which will be replaced in 2022 by Ariane 6), whose carrying capacity is however clearly superior. The China Rocket Co. has already successfully launched three satellites into orbit on board a Smart Dragon 1 rocket that blasted off in August 2019. In July 2019, the private Chinese company iSpace successfully launched a satellite, becoming the first private Chinese firm to achieve this.

The electric car industry is one that China has already dominated for years. Some 1.25 million electric cars found buyers in China in 2018, a world record representing more than half of global sales, according to the International Energy Agency (IEA). The Chinese leader in electric cars, BYD, beat America's Tesla with 248,000 units to 245,000.

---

[17] Xinhua, October 20, 2019.

The electric car fever is such that some 500 Chinese companies have jumped onto the bandwagon, supported by generous government grants aimed at reaching five million battery-powered, fuel cell and hybrid vehicles in 2020. At the end of 2018, the country had 342,000 charging stations, compared with 67,000 in the United States. Norway remains the world's champion in the adoption of electric cars with 58% of sales in March 2019 being electric vehicles against 4% in China. But when one says electric car one means batteries, and in this, China is by far the undisputed leader with two-thirds of the world production of lithium-ion batteries. The Chinese juggernaut CATL alone accounts for a quarter of the global offer, ahead of Japan's Panasonic, Chinese rival BYD and South Korea's LG-Chem. Europe is far behind with barely 1% of world production, while this market could reach 45 billion euros in 2027, of which 20–30% will be in Europe. Faced with China's domination in this strategic sector, Europe has finally reacted. In December 2019, the European Commission gave the green light to a project dubbed the "Airbus of batteries". The move authorizes seven countries already involved in this vast plan, including France and Germany, to provide 3.2 billion euros ($3.8 billion) in subsidies to a consortium of 17 companies to produce Li-ion batteries. The consortium members must for their part invest an additional five billion euros, making for a total of more than eight billion euros in investments in the coming years.

Overall sales of vehicles fell for the first time in decades in China in 2018, sliding by 3%. The drop was more dramatic in 2019, falling by 11% over the first eight months of the year. Sales of electric vehicles also suffered. This was due in no small part to the significant drop in government subsidies, which after reaching $58 billion in 2019, were due to completely disappear in 2020. While Europe and the United States are still trying to develop large-scale production of electric vehicles, China is one step ahead of Western competitors and looking at a different technology: the hydrogen fuel cell car. The technology consists of equipping a car with a tank of compressed hydrogen, which is transformed into electricity via a fuel cell to power an electric motor. The system, still in its infancy in Europe and the United States, offers the autonomy and refueling speed of gasoline and diesel cars, with the advantages of fully electric vehicles (silence and zero tailpipe emissions). "We have to create a hydrogen society," says Wan Gang, a vice chairman of the National Committee of the Chinese People's Political Consultative Conference (CPPCC), the body responsible for long-term strategic planning for China's economy. He was the man who two decades ago convinced the Chinese government to bet on electric vehicles. Even if sales of hydrogen vehicles still remain insignificant, due to both manufacturing costs and industrial obstacles, making it a national priority could help overcome those hurdles, he says. (Liu, Tian, Whitley *et al.*, 2019) The Chinese government had already invested $12 billion in the development of this new technology by June 2019. Beijing targets getting 5,000 hydrogen vehicles on the road in 2020, 50,000 by 2025 and one million in 2030.[18]

Civilian nuclear energy has recently become yet another area of excellence for Chinese industries. With help, especially from France, China has quickly integrated the latest nuclear power plant technologies and has now mastered the full range. China's civilian nuclear energy program started in 1985. As of the early 2000s, only three power plants had been built. It was only in 2005, under the leadership of then prime minister Wen Jiabao, that the country really started investing in this sector. Upon coming to power in 2012, Xi Jinping accelerated the process. While French companies pioneered the technology for the latest generation of reactors called European Pressurized Reactors (EPR), France's first EPR being built at Flamanville in

---

[18]China is not alone in the hydrogen car industry. A pioneer of this new technology, the Japanese giant Toyota, unveiled in early October 2019 its first hydrogen vehicle, the Mirai, which it plans to market at the end of 2020. Its Japanese rival Honda also unveiled a prototype, the Clarity, in the autumn of 2019. South Korea's Hyundai also has its ix35. Note that all these initiatives are being made by Asian carmakers. Germany's BMW announced in 2017 the launch of its first hydrogen car in 2021, a model which will however only be produced in limited numbers and whose ramp-up is not scheduled until 2025. On November 26, 2019, Swiss adventurer Bertrand Piccard set a distance record by traveling 778 kilometers on a single tank of hydrogen in a Hyundai Nexo.

Normandy has been beset by repeated technical delays to the point that its commissioning is now not foreseen until the end of 2022. But China, with little fanfare, connected the first EPR reactor, Taishan 1 in the southern province of Guangdong, to the grid in December 2018. Taishan 2 followed in September 2019. China could not have achieved this world premiere without the help of Framatome, France's civil nuclear energy development firm which is majority-owned by the nation's leading electricity firm, EDF. For its part, state-held EDF holds a 30% stake in the joint venture that built and operates the two 1,750 MW Taishan reactors. Chinese groups China General Nuclear Power Corporation (CGNC) and Guangdong Energy Group hold 51% and 19% stakes respectively. The entry into service of the Taishan reactors represents a real success for the French and Chinese nuclear industries. According to EDF, over 15,000 worked at the site at the peak of activity, including more than 200 French engineers. Some 40 French companies were involved. (Amalvy, 2019)

In 2019, China had around 46 reactors in operation. It is poised to surpass France and the United States with potentially 110 reactors in operation by 2030, thus becoming the top civil nuclear power in the world. China now exports nuclear power plants and is even beating its French, American and Russian competitors. Several Chinese plants are under construction in Pakistan. A third of the capital invested in the future Hinkley Point nuclear complex in the United Kingdom is of Chinese origin.[19] China will also provide power plants to Algeria, Argentina, Kenya, Romania, South Africa, Sudan and Turkey.

China is heavily dependent upon coal, a very polluting fuel, for its electricity production. In 2018, fossil fuels generated 71% of China's electricity, with coal accounting for around 67% and natural gas 4%. Hydroelectric accounted for about 19%, wind 5%, nuclear 4%, and solar and biomass the rest. The Chinese government is targeting a

---

[19] Although the British government welcomed this participation, since London joined the US position on the national security risk that telecommunications equipment from China's Huawei poses, concerns have been raised about China's role in the project.

nuclear capacity of 120,000 or even 150,000 MW by 2030, which would mean a tripling of the current generating capacity. China is also at the forefront of research into nuclear fusion, the holy grail of renewable energies. In November 2018, a Chinese reactor became the first to maintain for over a hundred seconds the conditions necessary for nuclear fusion, a major technological feat. The reactor, installed in Hefei in the eastern province of Anhui, performs experiments as part of the ITER project, the huge international nuclear fusion research project underway in southeast France. In 2017, the Chinese reactor had already broken the world record for maintaining the conditions necessary for nuclear fusion. Then in November 2019, it blew away its own record by reaching a temperature of 100 million degrees — six times the heat produced in the center of the Sun. The Experimental Advanced Superconducting Tokamak is better known by the acronym EAST. The tokamak uses powerful magnetic fields to contain the phenomenal heat needed to fuse atomic nuclei. Nuclear fusion should not be confused with fission, the division of atomic nuclei, which takes place in conventional nuclear power plants. Nuclear fusion is considered the energy of tomorrow because it is infinite, just like that of the Sun, and produces no pollution or long-lasting radiation. "We are hoping to expand international cooperation through this device (EAST) and make Chinese contributions to mankind's future use of nuclear fusion," said Song Yuntao, one of the top officials involved with the experimental reactor project. (Wang, 2019)

As part of the ITER program, France is currently building in the southern town of Saint-Paul-les-Durance a reactor that should reach 150 million degrees. Thousands of engineers and scientists have contributed to designing ITER since the idea of international collaboration on fusion energy was launched in 1985. ITER's member countries (China, the European Union, India, Japan, Korea, Russia and the United States) have engaged upon a 35-year project to build and operate the experimental facility. The first tests are not expected before 2025. In the meantime, China already has ambitions to build another nuclear fusion reactor which, unlike EAST, would be connected to the electrical grid and is hoped to start to supply electricity by mid-century, according to Song Yuntao. (*ibid.*) The planned budget for this post-ITER is 6 billion yuan ($914 million).

Another technological field where China has unabashedly overtaken its competitors is high-speed trains. In a period of ten years, China has built the largest high-speed rail network in the world. The Chinese rail giant China Railway Construction Corporation (CRCC) had in 2020 some 35,000 km of high-speed track, 21 times the French TGV network that was launched in the early 1980s, and two-thirds of all of the high-speed networks in the world. Where it used to take 24 hours to travel between Beijing and Shanghai in the old, drafty and uncomfortable railway cars, the new service called the *Fuxing Hao* or *Renaissance*, inaugurated in 2011, makes the 1,305-kilometer journey in 3 hours 58 minutes, traveling at an average of 329 kph, making this train the fastest in the world. The Chinese high-speed train has even established a speed record of 385 kph, in October 2019, on the new Beijing-Zhangjiakou line that was put into service at the end of 2019 in the northern Hebei province and which is the first automatic high-speed train line in the world.[20] Martin Raiser, the World Bank's country director in China, noted that:

> "China has built the largest high-speed rail network in the world. The impacts go well beyond the railway sector and include changed patterns of urban development, increases in tourism, and promotion of regional economic growth. Large numbers of people are now able to travel more easily and reliably than ever before, and the network has laid the groundwork for future reductions in greenhouse gas emissions." (World Bank, 2019)

The CRCC has also started the construction of a high-speed train line that will link Kunming in its southwestern Yunnan province to Singapore by 2026. It is a pharaonic project that extends over some 3,000 kilometers via Laos, Thailand and Malaysia. For the record, let us add that the United States does not have any high-speed train lines

---

[20] The world speed record belongs to Japan, with its Maglev (magnetic levitation) train which reached a speed of 603 kph on April 21, 2015. The Maglev is scheduled to enter service in 2027.

to date. Its sole high-speed rail project, between San Francisco and Los Angeles, has been abandoned. Meanwhile, China has started to export its high-speed trains. The latest example is the massive conglomerate Thai GP Group signing a $7.4 billion contract with CRCC for the construction of 220 kilometers of high-speed train lines to connect Bangkok's Suvarnabhumi and Don Mueang airports with the airport in the southern city of Pattaya, which is very popular among Western tourists. The construction of this network is set to start by the end of 2020. There is however a looming problem for China's railway adventure: the publicly-listed CRCC has accumulated a colossal debt of 5.4 trillion yuan ($823 billion) to carry out its program.

As Sino-American technological competition intensifies, the United States has increasingly spoken out about industrial espionage[21] and the looting of intellectual property. In July 2019, speaking before the US Senate Judiciary Committee, Federal Bureau of Investigation (FBI) Director Christopher Wray said there were more than a thousand open investigations into cases of suspected theft of intellectual property by Chinese companies, institutions and universities. "I would say that there is no country that poses a more severe counterintelligence threat to this country right now than China," he told lawmakers, adding that Beijing targeted all US industries. Reacting to these comments the following day, Chinese Foreign Ministry spokeswoman Hua Chunying flatly denied them as unfounded. "We don't steal, we don't rob, and we don't lie," she said. (*We don't steal*, 2019) The American administration estimates the damage caused by theft of intellectual property at $1.2 trillion for the period of 2014–2017 alone.[22]

---

[21] On the subject of Chinese espionage, the 2015 book by French journalist Roger Faligot: *Les services secrets chinois de Mao à nos jours* (Chinese secret services from Mao to the present day), has not become outdated in the least.

[22] BBC, November 8, 2019.

Chapter 5

The Military Domain: A Silent Rivalry Where America Remains in Control of the Game

The United States will remain the master of the world in the military domain for a long time to come. It is the only country capable of imposing its power simultaneously in all theaters across the planet. But China, a nuclear power since 1964 and with the world's second-largest defense budget, has for 20 years been engaged in the rapid modernization of its military. China has extended its territory far from its shores in the South China Sea and wants to control the Taiwan Strait, a strategic axis in international maritime traffic over which it asserts its sovereignty.

"When you have triumphed over an opponent, don't give in to the temptation to insult him on top of that. Don't laugh at your rivals, refrain from provoking them and, each time you win, be content with the pleasure of victory without glorifying yourself in words or deeds."

Jules Mazarin

Bréviaire des politiciens (Breviary of Politicians)

1864

In December 2019 US President Donald Trump signed a military budget of $738 billion for 2020, more than all the other countries of the planet put together. In all likelihood, the United States will continue to have the world's largest military budget over the coming decades. NATO expenditure amounted to $963 billion in 2018, under the combined effect of rising US military spending and the four-year effort, now clearly visible, by the 29 NATO allies of the United States to improve their "burden sharing", an oft-repeated demand made by Trump: for them to boost their defense expenditure. The American president opened the door to rearmament by designating China as the main threat to his country. At $682 billion in 2018, US military spending increased significantly for the first time since 2011 — a trend that continued in 2019 and in 2020. For British security and intelligence expert Charles Shoebridge, the record military budget of $732 billion in 2019 showed that Washington was preparing for conventional wars between states and not only to deal with terrorist groups. Following Donald Trump's promises, the US military benefited from a record budget allocation for 2019 with an increase of $50 billion over the previous year. The 2019 US military budget was approximately $30 billion more than the annual output of Switzerland, the world's 20th largest economy.

Now, to the next highest figures: Russia devoted to its military budget, according to figures from the World Economic Forum, the equivalent of $66 billion in 2015, whereas for France it was $55 billion. Russia was overtaken by France in 2018, at $51 and $56 billion respectively. In 2016, China was already in second place in the standings, up from sixth place in 2000. Its budget increased five-fold during that period, from $41 billion to $216 billion. That amount, which experts consider in reality to be underestimated by a wide margin,[1] makes China by far the most important military force in Asia. Its main rival, India, was in the sixth place, with a budget of nearly $57 billion, or only a quarter of that of China. The Chinese military budget has continued to grow. In 2020, it was 1.3 trillion yuan, a 6.6% increase from the previous year, although the lower value of the yuan made for a decline in dollar terms from 2016, to $178 billion.

---

[1] Western experts generally believe that China's actual military spending is 1.5-2 times the official budget, which in particular does not take into account the expenditure allocated to the development of new weapons.

The American military remains number one in the world not only in terms of its budget but also by its ability to deploy across the world. It has some 1.4 million men and women in uniform and has military bases on every continent. It owns the highest number of aircraft carriers in service, with 11 deployed in 2020. These are always accompanied by a flotilla of ten vessels (Aegis cruisers, destroyers, frigates, submarines and supply ships) which ensure their protection and logistical support. US combat groups can intervene quickly anywhere in the world.

But China will soon rank second in the world by the number of aircraft carriers. Its first, the *Liaoning*, an old ship bought second-hand from Ukraine and "retrofitted", has been operational since 2012. The second, the *Shandong*, completely designed and built in China, will be ready in 2020, and a third, already under construction, is intended to be put into service in 2025. Launched in December 2019, the *Shandong*, which displaces 50,000 tons, is longer than the *Liaoning* (315 meters long by 75 meters wide) and is capable of carrying 25 warplanes. These first two aircraft carriers are powered by conventional engines that produce dark exhaust trails that make them visible for miles around. "The primary purpose of this first domestic aircraft carrier will be to serve a regional defense mission. Beijing probably also will use the carrier to project power throughout the South China Sea and possibly into the Indian Ocean," the US Defense Intelligence Agency said in a 2019 report. (Axis, 2019b) But the third aircraft carrier will be nuclear powered and will thus be able to carry out missions that are significantly longer and further from China's shores. To date, only the United States and France have such ships. China will not stop there. By 2030, it could have three additional aircraft carriers.

The Chinese navy commissioned its first nuclear attack submarine in August 1974 and its first nuclear-powered ballistic missile submarine, a Type 092 christened the *406 Changzheng*, in March 1981. This entered service in 1987. The Chinese navy is now the second largest in the world in terms of tonnage, ahead of Russia, and the first in Asia with a total of 600 combat vessels. The People's Liberation Army (PLA) was estimated in 2015 to have 1.5 million men. After coming to power,

Xi Jinping very quickly embarked on a major modernization of the military which, under his aegis as the supreme leader of the Central Military Commission, launched an in-depth reorganization with a clear objective to strengthen the navy. On October 1, 2019, on the occasion of massive celebrations in Tiananmen Square for the 70th anniversary of the founding of the PRC, China for the first time exhibited its new intercontinental ballistic missile (ICBM), the Dongfeng 41, capable of carrying multiple nuclear warheads and boasting a range of 14,000 kilometers that puts the entire territory of the United States within its strike range. Experts estimate that in 2008 China had between 1,050 and 1,150 Dongfeng 15 and Dongfeng 11 short-range ballistic missiles deployed along its east coast, facing Taiwan, that are capable of carrying either conventional or nuclear payloads. The number has not ceased to increase since.[2]

If Beijing decides to launch a military operation against Taiwan, from the first second of the war until the moment the land invasion begins, "these missiles will scream toward the Taiwanese coast, with airfields, communication hubs, radar equipment, transportation nodes, and government offices in their sights." That is the scenario of Tanner Green, an American researcher specializing in East Asia geopolitics. Taken by surprise, American forces would require a certain amount of time before they could react and come to the assistance of the Taiwanese army.

> Concurrently, party sleeper agents or special forces discreetly ferried across the strait will begin an assassination campaign targeting the president and her Cabinet, other leaders of the Democratic Progressive Party, officials at key bureaucracies, prominent media personalities, important scientists or engineers, and their families. The goal of all this is twofold. In the narrower tactical sense, the PLA hopes to destroy as much of the Taiwanese Air Force on the ground as it can and from that point forward keep things chaotic enough on the ground that Taiwan's Air Force cannot sortie fast enough to challenge China's control of the air... Within a week (of the start of the land

---

[2] Beijing has also deployed on its eastern coast a vast network of ultra-sophisticated S-400 surface-to-air missile batteries that it has purchased from Russia.

invasion), they will have marched into Taipei; within two weeks they will have implemented a draconian martial law intended to convert the island into the pliant forward operating base the PLA will need to defend against the anticipated Japanese and American counter-campaigns. (Green, 2018)

A quick victory for the PLA over Taiwanese forces would follow, and the island would then be officially attached to the "motherland". It remains to be seen if the scenario would unfold in this manner quite so easily. Taiwan is in fact relatively well armed to defend itself. The United States, although it has recognized Beijing and one China, remains Taiwan's main supplier of weapons. Taiwan also bought from France in 1990 six Lafayette-class frigates, then, in 2012, sixty Mirage 200 fighter planes. That sale sparked a crisis between Paris and Beijing, so much so that no other country except the United States ventures to sell arms to Taiwan. Washington has nevertheless continued its deliveries of military equipment without heeding the threats of Chinese retaliation. Thus, on July 8, 2019, the US Department of Defense announced the sale to Taiwan of 108 M1A2 Abrams battle tanks and 250 short-range Stinger surface-to-air missile launchers, for a total amount of $2.2 billion. On August 21 of the same year, it approved the sale of 66 Lockheed Martin F-16 C/D Block 70 warplanes and 75 General Electric (GE) F110 engines, a transaction estimated at $8 billion. China may well protest vigorously, but in vain. According to the press release of the agency responsible for exports of US military equipment (the Defense Security Cooperation Agency): "The proposed sale of this equipment and support will not alter the basic military balance in the region." It added: "This proposed sale serves US national, economic, and security interests by supporting [Taiwan's] continuing efforts to modernize its armed forces and to maintain a credible defensive capability." The new F-16s "will help improve the security of the recipient and assist in maintaining political stability, military balance, and economic progress in the region." Taiwan's President Tsai Ing-wen said: "With strengthened defense capacities, Taiwan will certainly be better able to ensure peace and stability in the strait and in the region in the face of security challenges."

Would the Taiwanese army be able to resist a military confrontation with the PLA? This is an open question. It also remains to be seen what the level of US military support would be in the case of an armed conflict. Taiwan has for years maintained a defense industry active in most spheres. The defense budget announced for 2019 was 346 billion Taiwanese dollars (US$ 11.2 billion at the average 2019 exchange rate), or 2.16% of gross domestic product. Within this budget, 73.6 billion Taiwan dollars (an increase of 51.4% over one year) was to be devoted to projects involving indigenous weapons systems. The threat of a Chinese invasion is taken very seriously.

On August 2, 2019, the United States left the Intermediate-Range Nuclear Forces (INF) Treaty which it had signed with the USSR in 1987. This move will allow America to modernize its nuclear and conventional arsenal. One of the reasons for the withdrawal was American concerns about China, which was not a signatory to the treaty and therefore not subject to its constraints. A few hours after the American withdrawal, the Pentagon clearly announced its desire to surround China with missiles. Speaking to reporters on a trip to Australia, US Secretary of Defense Mark Esper said the Pentagon wanted to deploy intermediate-range missiles in the Pacific "sooner rather than later", adding he would prefer to do so within "months". He declined to say where they could be based, but the range of the missiles would put the Chinese coast and its Pacific islands at risk. On September 12, 2019, Secretary of the Army Ryan McCarthy drove home the point: these new missiles "will change the geometry within Southeast Asia". The day before, the US Marine Corps indicated that it had carried out a series of landing drills in hostile terrain and seizures of airstrips on the Japanese island of Iejima, off Okinawa, to demonstrate the capacity of the US military to invade a disputed island and establish a refueling site for air operations. "This type of raid gives [US] commanders in the Indo-Pacific region the ability to project power and conduct expeditionary operations in a potentially contested littoral environment," Major Anthony Cesaro of the 31st Marine Expeditionary Unit which conducted the exercise was quoted as saying on the Marine Corps website.

Meanwhile, on September 13, 2019, the American guided-missile frigate the USS *Wayne E. Meyer* cruised by the Paracel Islands to assert "freedom of navigation" rights in the area and dispute Beijing's claims on this archipelago. It was the sixth operation of that type in the first nine months of that year, compared with the eight in total made by the US Navy in 2017 and 2018. There had only been six during Barack Obama's entire presidency (2009–2017).

Less than a month after the death of the INF treaty, on August 19, 2019, the US announced it had tested a medium-range conventional missile from San Nicolas Island off California, which would have been banned under the pact. China was quick to react. The US test launch "will trigger a new round of the arms race, leading to an escalation of military confrontation, which will have a serious negative impact on the international and regional security situation," said Chinese foreign ministry spokesman Geng Shuang. (Lee, 2019) On September 4, 2019, the South Korean daily *Chosun Ilbo* revealed that the United States intended to begin deploying fifth-generation F-35A stealth fighters in the Asia-Pacific region in early 2020 and aimed to have 220 stationed there in 2025. A South Korean military spokesman quoted by the newspaper explained that "the United States considers the deployment of F-35s from a strategic perspective in the Asia-Pacific region to target not only North Korea but also China." South Korea has already received and deployed some of the first batch of 40 F-35As it ordered, with the first aircraft entering service in December 2019. (Gady, 2019) In September 2020 it was reported South Korea will buy another 20 F-35As and 20 F-35Bs (which offer short takeoff and vertical landing capability) for a light aircraft carrier it is planning. (Vavasseur, 2020) The United States has also installed an advanced anti-missile defense system in the Asia-Pacific region, the Terminal High Altitude Area Defense (THAAD) system in service since 2008 and with which South Korea is involved. This shield, designed to destroy medium or intermediate-range ballistic missiles, primarily aims to protect against missiles launched from North Korea but those from China as well.

The United States and its allies in the Pacific now have an impressive armada. Washington and Tokyo have notably set up on Japanese soil an elaborate system of radars, Japanese FPS-3 and FPS-5 models as well as the American FBX, capable of monitoring aircraft movements and possible missile launches in most of the East China Sea. The American military particularly fears China's intermediate-range Dongfeng 21 anti-ship ballistic missiles (DF 21) which can carry nuclear warheads. The two countries have in the area a fleet of fifteen destroyers equipped with Aegis Ballistic Missile Defense System air defense radars. Japan has in addition four AWACS aerial surveillance aircraft as well as ten P-1 anti-submarine maritime patrol planes. The United States meanwhile has eight of the latest-generation P-8 aircraft equipped with sonars capable of tracking Chinese submarines in the area. The US military has also developed a sophisticated system called the Towed Array Sensor System to ensure electronic surveillance in the East China Sea and the South China Sea. In this non-exhaustive list, the US also keeps the nuclear-powered aircraft carrier USS *Washington* and the flotilla that accompanies it in the region on a continuous basis, basing them at the Japanese naval base in Yokosuka, 65 kilometers south of Tokyo. In total, the US Navy has on a continuous basis around 34 destroyers, 17 nuclear missile submarines and two aircraft carriers in the area. (Holslag, 2015) The US military also has an airbase in Futenma, on the Japanese island of Okinawa, in the south of the Japanese archipelago, where U-2 reconnaissance planes take off to conduct specific surveillance missions in the area. All this without counting the American military installations established on the island of Guam, in the Pacific. The United States may further count upon the impressive Japanese navy, composed of ultra-modern vessels, and the Japanese air force, including in particular the 42 US-made multi-purpose F-35A Lightning II fighters it is in the process of acquiring.

China carried out its first nuclear bomb test on October 16, 1964, at the Lop Nor site in the northwestern Xinjiang region and its first H-bomb test on June 17, 1967. China's nuclear arsenal is not precisely known. According to Western estimates, in 2006 China had about 200 nuclear warheads, between 450 and 500 in 2007, and around 800 during the 2010s. A Russian general assessed China's nuclear arsenal at 1,600 to 1,800 warheads, while an American think tank spoke of 3,000 warheads in 2011. In comparison, the American arsenal is much larger. According to American scientists from the *Bulletin of the Atomic Scientists*, it contained at the beginning of 2019 some 3,800 nuclear warheads, of which 1,750 were operational, while the remaining 2,050 were held in reserve. Of these 1,750 nuclear warheads, 1,300 were placed on ballistic missiles, 300 at strategic bomber bases in the United States and 150 others at European bases.

Today, with the development of its Type 096 Tang-class submarine that will be capable of firing long-range JL-3 nuclear missiles that are believed to have a range of at least 8,000 kilometers, Beijing is acquiring a secure nuclear retaliatory strike capability that puts all major US cities under potential threat. During the Cold War, Moscow and Washington were conscious of the risks of nuclear escalation. Today, China and the United States are well aware of the fact that they must demonstrate restraint during a serious crisis and limit themselves to the use of conventional weapons lest they start a chain of events that leads to the total annihilation of their major cities. But during the Shangri-La Dialogue forum organized in Singapore from May 31 to June 2, 2019, the United States and China did not mince their words.

General Wei Fenghe, defense minister and one of the six members of the Central Military Commission, the highest Chinese representative ever to attend the Shangri-La Dialogue... delivered a speech [in the form of a warning] on fundamental Chinese interests. "As for the recent trade friction started by the US, if the US wants to talk, we will keep the door open. If they want a fight, we will fight till the end... If anyone dares to split Taiwan from China, the Chinese military has no choice but to fight at all costs for national unity." Acting US Defense Secretary Patrick Shanahan responded, without directly naming China, that "competition does not mean conflict," before adding that "behavior that erodes other nations' sovereignty and sows distrust of China's intentions must end." (Guibert, 2019)

China, the world's fifth-largest exporter of conventional weapons, is ready to sign "as soon as possible" the UN's Arms Trade Treaty, State Counselor and Minister of Foreign Affairs Wang Yi told the body on September 26, 2019. The United States is not a signatory.

The big question facing the countries in the Pacific allied with the United States is: has the US military kept its advantage over Chinese forces in the region? American and Western experts are beginning to doubt it has. Step by step, China has advanced its pieces, to the point of perhaps having gained the upper hand over its American adversary in the Pacific. For Francois Gere, historian and geostrategic specialist, and founding president of the French Institute for Strategic Analysis (IFAS):

> China's rise in military power is a recent phenomenon dating back about fifteen years… This transformation accompanies the new diplomatic posture of a China rising to the rank of the world's second power and resolutely turning to the open seas […] and towards exoatmospheric space where it positions its satellites while developing anti-satellite programs. Despite China's rising power it cannot pretend to compete with American capacities… In addition, throughout the Pacific region, the United States has strong allies like Japan, South Korea, Australia. China can only count upon itself. Under these conditions, while pursuing methodically its transformation, the PLA does not envisage a general confrontation for at least a generation. In naval aviation and space, US domination forbids any adventures. (Ces experts, 2019)

According to a February 2019 report from the Government Accountability Office (GAO), an agency of the US Congress that audits, investigates and evaluates the executive branch of government and its policies, the Army has made progress in "rebuilding readiness" but it still "faces challenges in staffing its evolving force structure, repairing and modernizing its equipment, and training its forces for potential large-scale conflicts". (Pendleton, 2019) The participation of the United States in various conflicts during the previous ten years, funding problems and a decline in numbers have resulted in a reduction in the combat ability of its troops, it found. Raising that level is a priority for Washington. The study highlights that the readiness of the American Army has been "degraded" by repeated deployments while the "adversaries" of the United States have improved their military potential.

More seriously, according to another report published in August 2019 by the United States Studies Centre at the University of Sydney entitled

"Averting crisis: American strategy, military spending and collective defence in the Indo-Pacific", the United States no longer has military preeminence in the Pacific. It even finds it difficult to defend its regional allies against China, whose influence continues to grow. "America no longer enjoys military primacy in the Indo-Pacific and its capacity to uphold a favorable balance of power is increasingly uncertain," said the report. (Townshend, Thomas-Noone & Steward, 2019) China's "growing" arsenal of missiles in the region threatens American bases and those of its allies, installations which "could be rendered useless by precision strikes in the opening hours of a conflict, the PLA missile threat challenges America's ability to freely operate its forces from forward locations throughout the region." (*ibid.*) All this despite the United States maintaining a lead in the fields of intelligence, ballistic missiles and latest-generation warplanes. China cannot count on alliances like those enjoyed by America, but its geographic location in the heart of the Pacific and its technological progress make it "a superpower that rivals the United States". (*ibid.*) "Chinese counter-intervention systems have undermined America's ability to project power into the Indo-Pacific, raising the risk that China could use limited force to achieve a *fait accompli* victory before America can respond; and challenging US security guarantees in the process." (*ibid.*) The report concludes the US military is "an atrophying force that is not sufficiently ready, equipped or postured for great power competition in the Indo-Pacific". (*ibid.*)

This assessment, if correct, would have serious consequences for the many allies of the United States, including Australia, Taiwan and Japan, which depend heavily upon American security guarantees.

> Faced with an increasingly contested regional security landscape and with limited defense resources at its disposal, the United States military is no longer assured of its ability to single-handedly uphold a favorable balance of power in the Indo-Pacific. China, by contrast, is growing ever more capable of challenging the regional order by force as a result of its large-scale investment in advanced military systems. (Townshend, Thomas-Noone & Steward, 2019)

The US military is in fact too dispersed across the world, while China has no global responsibilities and can thus concentrate its armed forces in the Pacific theater. As a result, Australia can no longer rely only on the United States for its security in the Pacific region and should strengthen its alliances to ensure "collective defense" by joining forces with those of allied nations such as Japan, the report concludes.

David Ochmanek, an analyst at the California-based RAND Corporation, also doubts the state of America's military power: "In our games, when we fight Russia and China, blue gets its ass handed to it." (Axe, 2019a) For Ochmanek, who spoke at a panel discussion at the Washington, DC-based Center for a New American Security in March 2019, US bases in the Pacific are vulnerable to attacks from Chinese long-range missiles. So too are large warships sailing the open seas. "Things that rely on sophisticated base infrastructure like runways and fuel tanks are going to have a hard time," Ochmanek said. "Things that sail on the surface of the sea are going to have a hard time." (*ibid.*)

China is now openly testing the reactions of US and allied forces in the Pacific. On July 23, 2019, four Chinese and Russian bombers led an unprecedented joint air exercise off the coasts of South Korea and Japan, a "massive development" in their bid to challenge US influence in the region, according to analysts quoted by Agence France-Presse. (China-Russia joint exercise, 2019) The exercise provoked protests from Seoul and Tokyo, which asserted that one of the two Russian aircraft violated its airspace. South Korean interceptors fired 400 warning shots after what Seoul said was a violation by the aircraft of a section of airspace near the Dokdo islets — controlled by South Korea but claimed by Japan as the Takeshima Islands. Tokyo said it had scrambled its jet fighters, and complained to Moscow. "It's a big deal because it displays confidence that the air forces of the two nations can coordinate a patrol of this nature in ways that the region will almost certainly find destabilizing," said Lyle Morris, a senior policy analyst at the RAND Corporation. China and Russia maintain increasingly close ties and have already conducted a number of joint military exercises.

But this joint air patrol had a particular purpose as it was carried out near disputed islands that are a source of diplomatic friction between Japan and South Korea. Ahn Chan-il, a North Korean defector who became a researcher in Seoul, considers the violation of airspace to have been "deliberate". "China and Russia are seeking to counterbalance Washington when it comes to North Korea's nuclear issues," he said. (*ibid.*) Adam Ni, a China researcher at Macquarie University in Sydney, said it was also significant that the bombers involved — two Chinese H-6Ks and two Russian Tu95s — are capable of carrying nuclear weapons. "So it's sending an additional message… that is a fairly massive development in terms of the regional security landscape," he said. (*ibid.*) In the opinion of several analysts quoted by AFP, cooperation between China and Russia goes well beyond the economic sphere and aims at becoming a broader partnership to overturn the status quo. "It also signals that Russian-PRC jointness has reached sufficient maturity that they can now conduct joint patrols," said J. Michael Cole, a Taipei-based senior fellow with the Global Taiwan Institute in Washington. "This, in my view, constitutes a direct challenge to the US alliance system in the Indo Pacific." (*ibid.*)

While some experts point the finger at the weakness of American forces in the Pacific, the US administration has moved swiftly since the beginning of 2020 to counter the rising strength of Chinese forces by rearming and aims to regain the advantage. The radical change in US strategy dates to the debate in the US Congress on the 2021 military budget. The budget proposal included the deployment of sea-to-surface and surface-to-surface Tomahawk missiles in the Asia-Pacific theater. The US military also plans to accelerate the deployment of a new generation of anti-ship missiles. One of the priorities in this new strategy is the planned use of small and mobile units of US Marines equipped with anti-ship missiles stationed in the western Pacific off Japan, Taiwan, the Philippines and Borneo. On March 5, 2020, Marine Corps Commandant Michael Berger told senators on the chamber's Armed Services Committee that these small teams armed with precision missiles could help US naval forces retake control of the seas off China. "The Tomahawk missile is one of the tools that is going to allow us to do that," he said. The sea-to-surface version of the missile that has been used since the 1991 Gulf War is to be updated and modified into sea-to-sea and surface-to-sea versions with a range of 1,600 kilometers. They are to undergo testing in 2022 to become operational in 2023, according to senior US military officials cited by Reuters. "The Americans are coming back strongly," the news agency quoted Ross Babbage, a former senior Australian government defense official, as saying. "By 2024 or 2025 there is a serious risk for the PLA that their military developments will be obsolete." (Lague, 2020)

Not being a signatory of the Intermediate-Range Nuclear Forces (INF) Treaty that prohibited the deployment by Russia and the United States of missiles with a range of 500 to 5,000 kilometers, China amassed a considerable arsenal of these missiles along its eastern coast. A portion of these target Taiwan. China has also equipped its ships and warplanes with highly sophisticated long-range missiles, in particular anti-ship missiles that could possibly wreak considerable damage on the vessels of the US 7th Fleet if a conflict breaks out. China's development and deployment of missiles during the past decade has given it a tangible advantage over US forces in the western Pacific, according to US military officials cited by Reuters. On the day following the March 2020 appearance by Marine Corps Commandant Berger before lawmakers, US Defense Secretary Mark Esper told journalists he intends to deploy land-based missiles in Asia in the next few months. The US Defense Department has $3.2 billion allocated in its budget for the development of long-range hypersonic missiles which would essentially be deployed in the Asian-Pacific theater. Potential targets would no doubt include the some 400 Chinese ships in the South China Sea, the East China Sea and the Yellow Sea.

The US military also plans to reinforce its position in the air in the region with the deployment of long-range B-21 stealth bombers that are due to enter service in the mid-2020s. It already has in the region B-1 bombers, which will soon be equipped with new anti-ship missiles with a range of 800 kilometers that will respond to an "urgent operational need", according to the US military's leader in the Pacific. The US Air Force and the Marines should receive 400 of these missiles by 2025, according to the Pentagon. "The US and allied focus on long-range land-attack and anti-ship cruise missiles was the quickest way to rebuild long-range conventional firepower in the Western Pacific region," Robert Haddick, a former US Marine Corps officer, told Reuters. (Lague, 2020) Haddick is the author of the prophetic 2014 book *Fire on the Water*, which sounded the alarm about the rising Chinese military strength in the region and its now dominant position against the United States. But for the moment, Japan, South Korea and the Philippines are all dragging their feet over agreeing to station US missiles on their territory.

The military rivalry between the United States on one side and China and Russia on the other also extends to space, raising the possibility of conflict far above the planet's surface — a prospect increasingly known as "star wars". On August 29, 2019, President Trump announced at an official ceremony the creation of a US "Space Command" charged with defending America's vital interests in space against threats posed by China and Russia. "This is a landmark day — one that recognizes the centrality of space to America's national security and defense," said Trump. This military command, SPACECOM, "will ensure that America's dominance in space is never questioned and never threatened, because we know the best way to prevent conflict is to prepare for victory," said Trump. China has already experimented with satellite-killer missiles. The first test took place on the night of January 11 to 12, 2007. A Chinese missile damaged an old Chinese weather satellite, a still operational Feng-Yun model located in a polar orbit 860 kilometers above the earth. For US intelligence services, it was a successful test of an anti-satellite weapon. The intermediate-range ballistic missile, launched from a site in the southwestern province of Sichuan, had a kinetic energy interceptor as its warhead. The United States and Russia had already conducted such tests. The next step would be satellite-killing satellites. China and Russia may have already succeeded in developing these without having deployed them in space. The US Space Command announced in July 2020 that it has evidence that Russia has tested a space-based anti-satellite weapon earlier that month. (Gohd, 2020)

On April 21, 2019, Donald Trump called Jimmy Carter to discuss China after the president of the United States from 1977 to 1981 wrote to him. Carter, later describing the conversation to a church congregation, said Trump expressed concern about how China is "getting ahead of us", which Carter agreed was true.

> "And do you know why? I normalized diplomatic relations with China in 1979. Since 1979 do you know how many times China has been at war with anybody? None. And we have stayed at war," he said... [Carter] called the United States "the most warlike nation in the history of the world," because of a tendency to try to force others to "adopt our American principles". Carter suggested that instead of war, China has been investing in its own infrastructure, mentioning that China has 18,000 miles of high-speed railroad. "How many miles of high-speed railroad do we have in this country?" Zero, the congregation answered. "We have wasted I think $3 trillion," Carter said of American military spending. "... It's more than you can imagine. China has not wasted a single penny on war and that's why they're ahead of us. In almost every way." (Hurt, 2019)

Chapter 6

The New Silk Roads: An Instrument of Chinese Expansionism

The pharaonic project called the Belt and Road Initiative, from which America is carefully excluded, is unprecedented in the contemporary history of China which over the ages has rarely ventured beyond its borders. A total of 138 countries have to date agreed to cooperate on this project with China, which intends to use it to expand its growing influence across the world. Xi Jinping has been forced to practice a certain caution, however, due to the growing resistance among some partners who now see it as an instrument of economic domination. If Central Asia remains the privileged neighborhood for Chinese investments, the entire world economy could ultimately be overwhelmed by Beijing's ambition.

"The sea was calm, but we could feel the discreet expansion of the flow that already covered the black palisades of the fishponds."

Jacques Chardonne

Les Destinées sentimentales (*Sentimental Destinies*)

Paris, Grasset, 1934–1936

The generic term "Silk Road" designates a certain number of routes that once linked China to the Roman Empire. Only China possessed, from the middle of the third millennium BC, the secrets of manufacturing silk, a soft, shimmering and resistant fabric that was highly valued in Europe. In addition to the trade in goods, the Silk Road also favored the exchange of beliefs and traditions. Legend has it that the art of unrolling the cocoons of silkworms (Bombyx mori) was discovered by an empress, the wife of the Yellow Emperor (Huangdi, the mythical ruler who supposedly governed from 2697 to 2598 BC) who is considered the father of Chinese civilization. The production of silk has always been entrusted to women. Disclosing its manufacturing secrets was punishable by death. Centuries later, those same silk threads had woven a vast commercial network linking China to Rome. The long and winding route that crosses northwest China has a rich history of more than two thousand years. The route starts from the ancient Imperial capitals of Luoyang and Xi'an, crosses the Yellow River in Lanzhou (western China) then enters the Gansu corridor, continuing along the edge of the desert and high mountain ranges. The trade flowed along it thanks to the merchants of Central Asia. Besides silk, they transported horses, cattle, hides and furs, as well as luxurious products such as ivory and jade. They also introduced new goods into China, such as cucumbers, nuts, sesame seeds, figs, alfalfa and pomegranates. And they brought new knowledge — including the art of producing wine by pressing grapes — which enriched the civilization of ancient China.

Stretching for thousands of kilometers, it is dotted with monuments and historical sites. The Silk Road of antiquity first referred to the old trade route that linked Central Asia to China. Originally, the Chinese traded in silk just within the borders of their empire. Their caravans traveled to the western confines of their territory, where they were often attacked by the peoples of Central Asia who coveted the valuables carried by the merchants. To protect the caravans, Emperor Wudi (141–87 BC) of the Han dynasty (206 BC–220 AD) sent General Zhang Qian (164–114 BC) on a mission to establish diplomatic relations with the small nomadic states along the border regions. General Zhang departed from Changsha, present-day Xi'an, then the capital of Han China, and led his troops to the vast areas of the west and then further into Central Asia. From then on, the merchants could safely develop the silk trade. It began to spread to other regions of the world as traders explored this new path. The period of greatest prosperity of the Silk Route was under the Tang dynasty which ruled from 618–907 AD. In the 11th century, the Mongols, then the masters of Asia, gave new impetus to the Silk Road, which had fallen into disuse after the expansion of the Arab world and Islam from the seventh century and the civil wars that ravaged China. The existence of the Silk Road was attested to by the Venetian Marco Polo who, in the 13th century, traveled to Mongolia to meet Emperor Kublai Khan, grandson of Genghis Khan. In *The Travels of Marco Polo*, he accurately recounted the existence of a road connecting Asia to Europe. But due to the increasing risks from the long distance traveled and more importantly due to the growing success of maritime transport, trade along this land route began to decline. While the Chinese continued to trade silk for furs with the Russians north of the original Silk Road, trade and traffic along this route had decreased significantly by the end of the fourteenth century.

The new Silk Road is much more ambitious. Called the Belt and Road Initiative (BRI) or One Belt One Road (OBOR), the project was announced in September 2013 by President Xi Jinping during a visit to Kazakhstan. Described by some as the biggest investment project since the Marshall Plan in the aftermath of World War II, the BRI is a colossal plan to build infrastructure such as ports, railways and roads all the way to the heart of the Mediterranean basin. It aims to allow China to source raw materials and especially to better penetrate the markets of the 138 Asian, African and European partner countries, which represent nearly 55% of global GDP, 70% of the world's population (4.4 billion people) and 75% of the world's energy reserves. The investment period for the BRI is about thirty-five years. The estimated cost of the first projects is around $900 billion. But the loans allocated by China to partner countries could reach the astronomical sum of $8 trillion.

The BRI also has a considerable impact on the environment, one that puts at risk the goal of limiting global warming to well below 2°C by 2100 as enshrined in the Paris Agreement. A study by the Tsinghua Center for Finance and Development estimates that the BRI's carbon footprint must be reduced by 68% to stay within the limit. The failure to do so would mean that the BRI projects alone would lead to warming of nearly 3°C. Among the projects that produce the most emissions are ports, pipelines, railways and highways. The greenhouse gas emissions of BRI signatory countries accounted for 28% of the global total in 2015. China's emissions accounted for another 30%.

Beyond the numbers and announcements, the BRI may signal a global trade revolution. It is in any case a formidable tool of political and economic domination. During the 19th CCP Congress in October 2017, Xi Jinping summarized the purpose of the initiative: "By 2050, China should rise to the top spot worldwide in terms of global power and international influence." Concretely, the BRI consists of two major international routes: one traces the line of the historic Silk Road entering China through Central Asia, and the other follows the sea routes from China to Southeast Asia, South Asia, Africa and Europe. In Asia, the BRI projects are financed by a dedicated institution: the Asian Infrastructure Investment Bank (AIIB) founded in 2012 and headquartered in Beijing. The AIIB has financed a large number of projects initiated by Chinese state-owned companies. Seven years after its launch, it has amassed an impressive portfolio. However, it remains an open question whether the BRI will unlock progress in signatory countries. Some partner countries question Chinese motives: Is the BRI a great demonstration of brotherly love or is it a hellish debt trap? Leaders of recipient countries are no doubt aware of, if not concerned about, the risk that the rise in their debt might make them so vulnerable that they may be forced to cede the infrastructure built to China and, along with it, part of their national sovereignty. But the BRI projects offer economic benefits that are immediate and tangible to countries in need of investment to unlock growth. High debt levels only pose possible risks at a later date.

In emerging Asian countries, where an estimated $1.7 trillion of infrastructure investment is required each year this decade, the BRI answers much of this financial need. The costs of some projects can be enormous in comparison to the size of local economies. Take for example the Laos-China railway. The construction of the line began in 2016 and was at that date the country's largest-ever foreign investment, equivalent to 35% of GDP. In Cambodia, Chinese investment triggered a construction boom to the tune of $18 billion in a country with a GDP of just over $22 billion. Myanmar in 2018 signed a contract worth $1.3 billion for the construction of a deep water port in the state of Rakhine which will link it to China and the East-West Economic corridor of five ASEAN countries. Burmese authorities support China's BRI strategy. Myanmar's State Counsellor Aung San Suu Kyi traveled to Beijing in May 2017 in order to participate in the Belt and Road Forum for International Cooperation, accompanied by the construction, transport and communications ministers. China finalized a $2 billion loan to Pakistan a few days after the election victory of Prime Minister Imran Khan in August 2018. (Carmona & Pham, 2019)

Pakistan, which is a partner in the massive $54 billion project to link China with the port of Gwadar that will provide Chinese firms easy land access to the Indian Ocean, was on the brink of insolvency in 2018. In early December 2018, the Pakistani government requested an emergency loan from the IMF. It reached a deal with the IMF the following year on a $6 billion loan, but disbursements were stalled when the government refused to implement certain reform measures. The COVID-19 pandemic worsened Pakistan's finances even further but the country was availing itself of debt restructuring measures offered by G20 countries in 2020. For its part, Malaysia has canceled three Chinese projects, including a railway line costing $20 billion, due to its inability to finance them. A Chinese project to build a spectacular highway linking the port of Bar, in Montenegro, to Serbia, and on which Chinese companies are carrying out 70% of the work, has plunged Montenegro into a level of debt that the IMF worries it will find difficult to repay: it now amounts to almost 80% of GDP. The list of beneficiary countries, all minority partners in these agreements, continues to lengthen. It also includes a large number of countries in Africa, Latin America and central and eastern Europe. The argument for taking on these loans remains simple: for many of these countries, access to international capital markets is difficult and China constitutes a "fraternal" source of capital. But these loans lead the most vulnerable countries into a trap of uncontrolled debt from which they can escape only by surrendering assets.

This is the notorious "debt trap" into which China's emerging nation partners are sinking. In fact, there are already many examples of trapped debtor countries. Sri Lanka provides one of the most striking. From 2010 to 2015, President Mahinda Rajapaksa oriented the country's policy in favor of China in exchange for major infrastructure programs under the BRI. But unable to meet its debt repayment obligations, Sri Lanka's next government was forced to cede to China the Hambantota deep water port as well as 6,000 hectares of adjacent land under a 99-year lease in exchange for writing off $1.1 billion in debt. It allowed for China to gain a foothold in the Indian Ocean, just a few hundred miles from India, its historic adversary. According to the Center for Global Development think tank, BRI loans have significantly increased the debt risk of eight already very indebted countries: Mongolia, Laos, the Maldives, Montenegro, Pakistan, Djibouti, Tajikistan and Kyrgyzstan. Emmanuel Macron, at a summit with Xi Jinping in January 2018, stated that the new Silk Roads "must not become roads of a new hegemony that places the countries they cross into vassalage".

An October 2019 study by the Lowy Institute, an independent Australian international policy think tank based in Sydney, warned that for small South Pacific states such as Papua New Guinea and Vanuatu, also BRI partners, there is an increasing risk of falling into a state of dependence on China as they find themselves unable to repay mountains of debt contracted from Beijing. Between 2011 and 2018, China allocated loans totaling $6 billion to these small countries, or the equivalent of 21% of the region's GDP. The bulk of these loans, $4.1 billion, went to Papua New Guinea. China has during this period become the largest creditor to Tonga, Samoa and Vanuatu. "The sheer scale of China's lending and its lack of strong institutional mechanisms to protect the debt sustainability of borrowing countries pose clear risks," the study found. (Rajah, Dayant & Pryke, 2019) The South Pacific has been a theater of intense competition between China, the

United States and Australia for several years, with each trying to strengthen its geostrategic influence there. China has embarked on a policy of active seduction of these countries which have rich fishing grounds and are located along strategic maritime routes, with high-ranking officials making numerous visits. Six countries in the region are currently indebted to Beijing: the Cook Islands, Fiji, Papua New Guinea, Samoa, Tonga and Vanuatu.

In May 2019, Italy signed a memorandum of understanding with China, thus becoming the first G7 country and EU founding member to join the BRI. This agreement, negotiated by Italy in secret over many months without consulting its EU partners, was concluded during an official visit by Xi Jinping. It offers Chinese companies privileged access to four Italian ports, the electricity market and to the defense contractor Leonardo. Italy thus gave the BRI an entry point into Europe. Specifically, the ports of Genoa and Trieste joined forces with state groups China Communications Construction Company (CCCC) and China Merchants, which take over part of their operations. Those of Palermo and Ravenna forged partnerships with Chinese shipping companies. "Our ports will become the European terminals of the new Silk Road," Prime Minister Giuseppe Conte rejoiced. (Zaugg, 2019) Beijing hopes to gain faster access to the markets of central and northern Europe by shipping its products through Mediterranean ports that are linked to the rest of the continent by rail and road. China scored a huge political victory by signing the agreement with Italy as it drove a wedge into the G7 camp. "This is a major diplomatic coup for China," said Jan Weidenfeld of the Mercator Institute for China Studies. "Italy becomes the first country in the G7 and the first founding member of the European Union to officially support the One Belt, One Road project." (Zaugg, 2019)

The European Union is obviously concerned, but having nothing to offer as an alternative, has been a helpless spectator to the progress made by China at the heart of Europe. Reacting to this agreement, President Emmanuel Macron declared: "The time for European naivete has passed. For many years we have had an uncoordinated approach and China has taken advantage of our divisions." According to the economist Jean-Paul Tchang:

> The Italians see a way to breathe life into the once glorious pavilion of Trieste, and to catch up to Germany, England and France in the export of products to China. Yet conceding the port constitutes de facto an abandonment of sovereignty. Conceded freely without the need to use force. The Chinese are masters in the theory of the Art of War from their ancestral traditions which they have brought up to date with Xi Jinping's affable smile. (Questions, 2019)

Several European countries such as Croatia, the Czech Republic, Slovakia, Hungary, Bulgaria, Romania, Portugal and Malta have already signed similar agreements. But as Steve Tsang, director of the Chinese Institute of SOAS University of London underlines, "they do not have the same symbolic weight as Italy". At the Indo-Pacific Business Forum in July 2018, US Secretary of State Mike Pompeo announced the upcoming launch of an infrastructure development plan in Asia, under which the United States was expected to invest $113 billion. This program was a rather feeble response from Washington to China's BRI. The United States has, on several occasions, severely criticized the BRI and warned countries interested in joining it against the possible risks of unsustainable debt.

Yves Carmona and Minh Pham point out that in Europe "Chinese BRI investment has pushed forward apace". Greece was one of the first targets in Europe. In 2016, Greece concluded an agreement under which it conceded to China for $1.7 billion the management of two of the three terminals in Piraeus, the historic Athens port which is the largest in the country. China has also set its sights on:

> ...similar installations in Spain, Portugal, Malta and Cyprus, which create a maritime value chain that develops a position of strength in the Mediterranean. If this nautical connectivity serves its interests, it also creates a fault line within the EU. It sets member states from the west and the north, who see the BRI as a Trojan horse — dangerous beneath its harmless exterior — against those of the south, the center and the east who welcome the initiative. Thus, in 2017, this fault line led Greece to block an EU declaration at the United Nations

criticizing Chinese human rights policy… All in all, the reality is that the West as a whole is unable to find an effective strategy, commensurate with the overall challenge posed by China. Apart from denouncing the BRI initiative as a debt trap by extolling the virtues of austerity and budgetary rigor, the response of the United States, the EU and others has been simply too little, too late and too ineffective. In this undeclared war they must confront China in the absence of demarcated front lines, policies and budgets that are clearly aggressive, and a visible target to shoot at. At the moment, the West is struggling. (Carmona & Pham, 2019)

The European Union is not standing still, however. It now seeks to demonstrate a new unity and to speak with one voice so that it can stand up to both China and the United States. This is why during his official visit to China in November 2019, Emmanuel Macron added to his official delegation a German minister and a European commissioner. In March 2019, on the occasion of a visit to France by President Xi Jinping, Macron had at his side Chancellor Angela Merkel and the head of the European Commission, Jean-Claude Juncker. In 2020, during the German presidency of the European Union, Angela Merkel organized a summit of the 27 member states with the Chinese president, which was held via video conference due to the COVID-19 pandemic. Already a year earlier, Merkel had called on EU members to align their policies towards China, warning of the "disastrous effects" of acting alone in these times of tensions over human rights and telecommunications technology. "One of the biggest dangers… is that individual countries in Europe will have their own policies towards China and then mixed signals will be sent out," she told German lawmakers. "That would be disastrous not for China but for us in Europe," Merkel added. (Merkel calls for Europe, 2019)

The EU is also looking to Japan for a response to the BRI and as a counterweight to China. This is why in September 2019 Jean-Claude Juncker and Japanese Prime Minister Shinzo Abe signed at an EU-Asia Forum in Brussels a vast agreement aimed at coordinating new transport networks as well as new energy and digital infrastructure linking Europe to Asia, with 60 billion euros ($71 billion) of investments backed by EU guarantees, development banks and the private sector.

"The agreement stresses the importance of implementing 'sustainable' projects, on both an environmental and financial level... Connectivity must also be financially sustainable. It's about bequeathing to generations to come a more interconnected world, a cleaner world without mountains of debt," Juncker said, in a thinly-veiled allusion to China's BRI. (L'UE et le Japon, 2019) "It's also about creating more interconnections between all countries around the world and not more dependence upon a single country," he added. (*ibid.*) "Whether it be a single road or a single port, when the EU and Japan undertake something, we are able to build sustainable, rules-based connectivity from the Indo-Pacific to the Western Balkans and Africa," Abe told the forum. (Emmot, 2019)

While the EU had been fairly timid when faced with China, it has begun to speak with one voice and in the summer of 2020 adopted a harder tone that shows it seeks to take its place in the triangular China-US-EU game. When addressing Chinese President Xi Jinping on June 22 at the EU-China summit, held over video conference, EU Commission chief Ursula von der Leyen acknowledged that EU-China relations were "challenging" and "complex". She accused Chinese authorities of not having honored their promises in terms of protecting EU investments in China, respecting human rights and climate change. She called the EU's relationship with China "one of the most strategically important and one of the most challenging" it has. Von der Leyen also pointed to a rise in online disinformation emanating from China as well as cyberattacks on hospitals and dedicated computing centers. "We pointed out clearly that this cannot be tolerated," she said. Von der Leyen also called for "more ambition on the Chinese side in order to conclude negotiations on an investment agreement." None of these remarks were included in the information provided by official Chinese news publications. Instead, they focused on comments by Xi Jinping, who was clearly trying to minimize the differences between Beijing and Brussels. "China wants peace instead of hegemony," he said. China is a "partner not an opponent" of the European Union and will continue its reforms and opening up, which will provide Europe with new opportunities for cooperation and development. "Whatever the international changes, China will take the side of multilateralism and adhere to the concept of global governance," said Xi. Addressing Chinese Prime Minister Li Keqiang, European Council President Charles Michel said, "We have to recognize that we do not share the same values, political systems, or approach to multilateralism." The tone was clearly different from that previously adopted by EU officials. While not wanting to jump into the camp of the United States, from which it plans to keep its distance, the EU is clearly indicating it intends to join the great game underway between the United States and China. The statements came only days after the presentation of a white paper by European Commission Vice President Margrethe Vestager and Internal Market Commissioner Thierry Breton that should by the end of 2020 see the EU finally put in place effective protection for European companies from unfair takeovers by state-subsidized firms.

Chapter 7

Space: A New Target for Conquest

The United States maintains a significant lead in the conquest of space, but China dreams of walking among the global giants in an area where it was barely present 20 years ago. This chapter compares NASA's new goals, including the help it receives from the private sector, to the ambitious Chinese program. The Americans are aiming for a return to the Moon and the conquest of Mars.

"Space is ours, as long as we know how to observe it."

Alain Ayache
Editor, businessman

The United States remains by far the world's leading space power. Many still remember the extraordinary feat of sending the first men to the moon aboard a Saturn V rocket on the famous Apollo 11 flight. On July 20, 1969, the whole world witnessed live on television astronaut Neil Armstrong step onto the Moon and heard the most famous quote of the twentieth century: "One small step for (a) man, one giant leap for mankind." Last year America and the world enthusiastically celebrated the fiftieth anniversary of this space epic, an achievement that restored prestige to the United States during the Cold War against the Soviet Union which had taken an early lead in space.

In 2020, the United States along with Russia and China remain the only three countries to have mastered sending human beings into space. The United States has the largest network of satellites to monitor the whole planet, an undeniable advantage in times of war and in times of peace. Currently, some 1,500 civilian and military satellites streak above our heads in orbits that are low, medium, high or geostationary. There will be 6,000 in five to ten years' time. Since 2000, the United States alone accounted for more than 90% of global military space spending. Since 2001, and the coming to power of the Bush administration, the United States has made new efforts to dominate space. Space is a major element of the US understanding of national security and supremacy, from both military and technological aspects, which are summed up in the doctrines of "Space Control" and "Space Dominance". (Villain, undated) In March 2019, the administration of President Donald Trump announced an acceleration of the US space program with a return of American astronauts to the Moon no later than 2024. NASA had until then considered a return to the Moon impossible before 2028. Then at a July ceremony commemorating the 50th anniversary of the Apollo 11 mission at the White House, Donald Trump announced that a new Moon landing would be just a step towards sending astronauts to Mars. "To get to Mars, you have to land on the Moon, they say," Trump said in the Oval Office, flanked by Buzz Aldrin and Michael Collins, the two Apollo 11 astronauts still alive (Neil Armstrong died in 2012). At the beginning of July, Trump had already warned in a tweet: "For all of the money we are spending, NASA should NOT be talking about going to the Moon — We did that 50 years ago. They should be focused on the much bigger things we are doing, including Mars (of which the Moon is a part), Defense and Science!" NASA then stated that the plan was to go to the Moon in 2024, and then Mars the following decade. The United States has given a name to its lunar program: Artemis. Simultaneously, President Trump promised an extra $1.6 billion to NASA to ensure that the target date of 2024 is met. For this mission, Boeing is in charge of developing a new giant rocket, the SLS (Space Launch System), which test-fired the booster in September 2020. Private companies including Blue Origin and Space X are among the firms designing crewed lunar landers.

American private companies are heavily involved in the renewed US push into space, in particular SpaceX (officially Space Exploration Technologies Corporation) which is owned by American billionaire

Elon Musk. He published the first photo of the new Starship launcher in September 2019 and tweeted: "Starship will allow us to inhabit other worlds." The SpaceX CEO has great ambitions for the conquest of space, including putting men on the Moon and then heading to Mars. At the end of 2018, he announced the name of the first man the company will send into orbit around the Moon: Japanese billionaire Yusaku Maezawa. SpaceX employs over 7,000 people, primarily in California. It has two launch facilities at Cape Canaveral in Florida, one at Vandenberg Air Force Base in California, plus another that is under construction in south Texas at Boca Chica. The United States had not sent a man into space using one of its own launchers since the end of the space shuttle program in 2011, but on October 10, 2019, NASA chief Jim Bridenstine declared that SpaceX's Crew Dragon capsule would be able to send an astronaut into Earth orbit during the first quarter of 2020. His forecast was off just slightly, SpaceX accomplished the first manned private space flight on May 31 when two astronauts blasted off for the International Space Station in their Crew Dragon capsule atop a SpaceX Falcon 9 rocket. This historic achievement also had very important practical implications for the United States — it ended the country's nearly 10-year complete dependence upon the Russians to launch astronauts to the ISS due to the abandonment of the space shuttles. Meanwhile, on October 19, 2019, NASA carried out the first spacewalk conducted exclusively by women. Christina Koch and Jessica Meir spent seven hours outside the International Space Station. The US military also has a spacecraft, the X-37B, which performs covert missions in orbit around the Earth. On October 27, 2019, the unmanned vehicle, built by Boeing, returned to earth after a 780-day mission, breaking its own record for time spent in orbit. The US Air Force has never explained the purpose of these missions. As for other ongoing missions, it is impossible not to marvel at the extraordinary epic of NASA's twin probes, Voyager 1 and Voyager 2, which were launched on September 5, 1977. Having flown past Jupiter, Saturn, Uranus and Neptune, they have now left our solar system and entered interstellar space. Both probes have traveled billions of kilometers, but still continue to transmit precious scientific data.

In October 2019, NASA chief Bridenstine invited Europe to participate in its lunar program, thus opening up the opportunity for non-Americans to set foot on lunar soil. "I think there's lots of room on the Moon, and we need all our international partners to go with us to the Moon," he told a press conference on the first day of the 70th International Astronautical Congress, a major annual meeting of the space world. "If we can come to agreements on the contributions of all the nations and how they're going to be a part of the architecture, then certainly I would, I would see that there'd be no reason we can't have all of our international partners with us on the Moon," he added. (NASA wants international partners, 2019)

The following month ministers from the 22 member states of the European Space Agency (ESA) answered with a resounding yes and committed to investing several hundred million dollars in the Artemis project. During the same meeting in the Spanish city of Seville, they adopted a sharply higher budget of 14.4 billion euros ($17.1 billion) for the 2020–2025 period — an unparalleled amount since the founding in 1975 of the intergovernmental organization — so that Europe can take its place in the effort. "We are in discussion also with NASA, so that we have European astronauts on the surface of the Moon — this is of course the European intention," ESA chief Jan Wörner said at the same October press conference at which Bridenstine unveiled the offer. "2024 is for sure something which is purely American," Wörner later told AFP. For Europeans, it could be "2027, 2028, something like that". Meanwhile, Hiroshi Yamakawa, president of the Japanese space agency JAXA, said: "It's a very simple question to me because JAXA would like to send Japanese astronauts to the surface of the Moon" (NASA wants international partners, 2019).

The United States also received unexpected support from Australia. Prime Minister Scott Morrison announced his country wanted to participate in the new American lunar adventure and offered to contribute $101 million during a visit to Washington on September 22, 2019.[1]

---

[1] The announcement was made during Morrison's visit to NASA headquarters in Washington.

Finally, we can't forget the existence of the International Space Station (ISS) which brings together fifteen countries (the United States, Russia, Japan, Canada and 11 European countries):

> ... with a mass of 420 tons, a surface area of 108 by 73 meters, and a price tag of about $150 billion, it is the largest orbiting structure in the history of the world... Its construction began on November 20, 1998, when a Russian Proton rocket launched into orbit the Zarya ("Dawn") module. Three weeks later, the space shuttle Endeavor lifted into space the first American module, the Unity junction node, and assembled the two elements. The third module, Zvezda ("Star"), arrived in July 2000 and paved the way for permanent human occupation which began on November 2, 2000... Since its creation, 140 launches have participated in the construction and occupation of the International Space Station. To date (early December 2013), 91 Russian launches have taken place, mainly to send manned Soyuz or Progress cargo vessels, but also to deliver the Russian modules to the station. Space shuttles have visited the ISS 37 times and played an instrumental role with its higher payload capacity than other vessels (Esslinger, 2019).

Despite the renewed focus on the Moon, NASA is not neglecting Mars. On July 30, 2020, it launched the Perseverance Mars Rover, which should touch down on the red planet in February 2021. The mission aims to address the dizzying question: has life existed anywhere besides Earth? The rover should land in the 45-kilometer-wide Jezero crater. "We know that a little more than three billion years ago, it was where a river delta emptied into a lake," says Jean-Yves Le Gall, the head of France's CNES national space research institute. In another first, Perseverance will drill into the Martian soil. It will take samples of approximately 15 grams each and then hermetically seal them into tubes using a sophisticated robotic system. At the end of the mission, the 350–500 grams in collected samples will be left on the surface for retrieval by a mission planned for around 2030 that will take them back to Earth.

China is not remaining on the sidelines in the race to Mars. On July 23, 2020, it successfully launched Tianwen-1 on a Long March 5 rocket for a seven-month journey there. "As a first try for China, I don't expect it to do anything significant beyond what the US has already done," said Jonathan McDowell, an astronomer at the Harvard-Smithsonian Center for Astrophysics. (Ehret, 2020) Yet in its first mission, China aims to achieve everything that NASA has achieved over several forays to Mars since the 1970s: place a probe into orbit, set down a lander, deploy a remote-controlled rover to carry out experiments on the surface. "As long as (Tianwen) safely lands on the Martian surface and sends back the first image, the mission will... be a big success," said Chen Lan, an analyst for the Go-Taikonauts.com website that specializes on the Chinese space program. (*ibid*.) The mission was named Tianwen-1, or Questions to Heaven, in homage to an ancient Chinese poem that touches upon the cosmos. The mission's rover, which weighs over 200 kilograms, has four solar panels and six wheels and is planned to be operational for three months. Among its missions: to conduct analyses of the soil and atmosphere, take photos, and contribute to the ongoing effort to map the planet.

On January 3, 2019, China became the first country to land on the far side of the Moon, ten years after the first spacewalk by a taikonaut, as Chinese astronauts are known. The space probe Chang'e 4, named after the Moon goddess in Chinese mythology, entered lunar orbit on December 13, 2018. It made a soft landing two weeks later in the Von Karman crater located in the South Pole-Aitken basin, a technological feat that was praised around the world. This was the eighth Chinese spacecraft sent to the Moon and the second to land there. Chang'e 4 featured a lander and a rover that conveyed to the astonished world in the fall of 2019 some startling shots from this little-known part of the Moon. On November 23, 2020, the Chang'e 5 mission got underway to collect lunar rock samples and return them to Earth. Launched atop a Long March 5 rocket, the most powerful ever launched by China, the mission was set to gather more than just surface soil with its robotic arm. It was also equipped with a drill to obtain samples from as far down as two meters. After having collected the samples the lander needs to return to orbit and then package and transfer the samples to a capsule that will protect them from the high temperatures during entry into Earth's atmosphere. If the mission is a success it will be one steeped in symbolism, as it will make China just the third nation to accomplish such a feat after the United States and the Soviet Union, which did it with its Luna-24 module in 1976. A success would provide valuable information about the Moon's history and valuable technical experience that will further Chinese efforts towards manned missions to the Moon. The Chinese space program has clearly closed some of its gap with the United States. This is despite a still modest budget of $8.4 billion in 2017. It may be the second largest space budget in the world, but the US government spent $48 billion on its civil and military space programs that year.

China launched its first satellite, the *Dongfanghong 1*, aboard a Long March rocket in 1970. This was a propaganda satellite that broadcast the Maoist national anthem of the time, *The East is Red*, and was placed in orbit 13 years after the Soviet Union put the first satellite, *Sputnik*, in orbit on October 4, 1957. In October 2003, Yang Liwei became the first taikonaut. He circled the Earth fourteen times in 21 hours. In September 2008, China carried out a spacewalk for the first time. In October 2016, China dispatched two taikonauts to its orbital laboratory for a record thirty days in space. The mission's goal was to prepare for the deployment by 2022 of the first Chinese manned space station. In April 2018, the Chinese space agency said: "We believe that the Chinese nation's dream of living one day in a lunar palace could become a reality." This moon base would be composed of several cabins linked together and filled with oxygen so that human beings could inhabit it. This base is envisaged around 2035. The purpose of the inhabited lunar base would be to "conduct further research on the Moon and explore ways to harness the resources there," Wang Lisheng, a member of the Chinese Academy of Engineering, explained in October 2018. "This installation will make it possible to acquire experience which will be extremely useful for the development of manned missions on Mars," he added. (Arzt, 2018)

In June 2019, China launched a Long March 11 rocket from a shipping platform in the Yellow Sea off the coast of the eastern province of Shandong, placing into orbit seven satellites. This success makes China the third country, after the United States and Russia, to have successfully placed satellites into orbit with rockets launched from a floating platform. The technique allows for launches closer to the equator that are more efficient. The next steps are as follows: in 2020, the Chang'e 5 mission should allow the collection of two kilograms of lunar rocks in the Ocean of Storms and bring them back to Earth; in 2023, in a partnership with France, the Chang'e 6 mission will collect samples from both sides of the Moon; in 2030, China will send robots that will explore both poles of the Moon before starting manned missions in 2036. Eventually, China intends to establish a permanently occupied lunar base. In 2019, China became the top country in the world in the number of satellite launches with 34 (32 successful), ahead of the United States with 27. Forty are planned for 2020.

In the meantime, not all countries have succeeded in their lunar missions. In September 2019, India, another competitor in the space race, failed to successfully land the Chandrayaan-2 robot near the south pole of the Moon. Contact with the Vikram probe was lost only a few moments before landing. In April 2019, an Israeli probe, crashed while attempting to land on the Moon. Japan, for its part, achieved a real technological feat in July 2019 by successfully landing the probe Hayabusa 2 on the asteroid Ryugu which revolves around the Sun some 340 million kilometers from Earth. This delicate mission, which began in 2014, aimed to enrich knowledge on the formation of our solar system.

Meanwhile, China has deployed a network of satellites that will serve as an indigenous navigation system: the BeiDou Navigation Satellite System. After having placed the final satellite in orbit in mid-2020, BeiDou has global coverage and will compete with the American Global Positioning System (GPS) network, Russia's GLONASS and Europe's Galileo network which was expected to have a full complement of satellites operating at the end of 2020.

Chapter 8

Obstacles to Chinese Supremacy

C hina is located in the heart of the Asia region which has become the economic center of gravity of the planet. But there are factors that hinder China's further development: the environment, demography, and a corrupt totalitarian regime that may yet find itself unable to contain aspirations for more democracy despite at least temporarily tamping down unrest in Hong Kong with draconian legal measures. China will encounter major difficulties in becoming the dominant power in the world, while the United States has a significant lead that ensures it will retain the top ranking for some time to come.

"All falls call for compassion and forgiveness, except those that disguise themselves as ascents."

Gustave Thibon

L'Équilibre et l'Harmonie (Equilibrium and Harmony)

Paris, Fayard, 1976

Asia has surpassed the West as the leading economic hub. The region is already home to more than half of the population of the globe. Twenty-one of the thirty largest cities on the planet are in Asia, according to United Nations data. In 2020, Asia was set to become home to half of the world's middle class with an income between $10 and $100 per day in purchasing power parity. (Romei & Reed, 2019) According to the United Nations Conference on Trade and

Development (UNCTAD), Asian economies combined overtook the rest of the world in terms of GDP in purchasing power parity in 2020, while they represented only a third in 2000. In the 21st century we are living in the age of Asia. It has been an astonishing swing of the pendulum, with China driving the change.

On November 15, 2020, 15 Asian-Pacific countries signed the Regional Comprehensive Economic Partnership (RCEP). Largely driven by China, the free-trade agreement creates the world's largest trading bloc as the signatory countries and their 2.2 billion inhabitants account for 30% of global GDP. The RCEP includes ten ASEAN states: Brunei, Cambodia, Indonesia, Laos, Malaysia, Myanmar, the Philippines, Singapore, Thailand, and Vietnam; plus Australia, China, Japan, New Zealand, and South Korea. The United States was not part of the deal, which is yet another example that the world's economic center of gravity has shifted to Asia. Amid questions over Washington's engagement in Asia, the RCEP may cement China's position more firmly as an economic partner with Southeast Asia, Japan and Korea, putting the world's second-biggest economy in a better position to shape the region's trade rules, observers said. The signature of the RCEP follows the abandonment of the Trans-Pacific Partnership (TPP) by Donald Trump at the start of his presidency in January 2017, leaving the world's biggest economy out of two trade groups that span the fastest-growing region on earth. Chinese Premier Li Keqiang said, "The signing of the RCEP is not only a landmark achievement of East Asian regional cooperation, but also a victory of multilateralism and free trade... and provides new impetus to the recovery of world economic growth."

And while China retains gigantic reserves of strength, it now faces major obstacles to its further development. The first of these obstacles is to be found in the field of the environment and in the considerable damage inflicted by the unsustainable pace of its economic growth. In August 2019, the Intergovernmental Panel on Climate Change (IPCC), which brings together delegations from 195 countries, sounded the alarm on soil depletion. On the sidelines of an IPCC meeting in Geneva, Olivier De Schutter, a former UN rapporteur, called for a change in the world's agricultural model. He emphasized that:

> China faces a serious problem with desertification and soil depletion. This factor, and the impatience of the population in the face of air pollution, led to including the notion of "ecological civilization" in its constitution. China is afraid: it must feed 20% of the world's population with less than 9% of the world's arable land even as the emergence of a middle class and associated changes in eating habits along with urbanization increases pressure on resources. We can therefore express the hope that Qu Dongyu, the new Director-General of the FAO, will be sensitive to the urgency of a transition to agroecology, as his predecessor José Graziano da Silva himself finally recognized. (Foucart, 2019)

China remains the biggest polluter on the planet, the top greenhouse gas emitter. China consumes more resources than all the other countries of the world combined. A fact that is felt every day in major cities across the country. In 2014, the Chinese authorities declared war on pollution. "We must firmly establish this concept of a socialist ecological civilization. Develop a harmonious relationship between man and nature and do everything to protect the environment for future generations," proclaimed President Xi Jinping. It has achieved some initial results. China has gradually become the world champion of green energy. At the end of April 2019, the 63rd offshore wind turbine was placed in the China Sea off the eastern province of Zhejiang. The project mobilized 600 million euros in investments ($710 million) and boasts a capacity of 252 MW, enough to power 250,000 homes. China adds the equivalent of a football pitch of solar panels every hour. The world's largest floating solar power plant at roughly a quarter of the surface area of Manhattan is located near Shanghai. The sector is heavily subsidized: five euro cents is paid to the producer for each kW of electricity generated on top of the negotiated sale price.

Meanwhile, massive deforestation has occurred over the past forty years due to industrialization and the expansion of urban areas, as well as illegal logging, especially in Tibet.[1]

---

[1] According to a white paper on ecology produced by the Tibetan Central Administration in exile that was published in December 2018, the wooded areas of

[Despite this,] China is now the country that plants the most trees in the world thanks to the reforestation project started in the 1970s. The aim is to create by 2050 the "Green Great Wall" of China, the largest artificial forest in the world, to reduce pollution and stop the advance of the Gobi Desert, which the Chinese have come to call the "yellow dragon". Indeed, the risk is that it spreads further along with the development of urbanization and intensive agricultural areas, as temperatures climbed by two degrees in five years in the north of the country. More than 66 billion trees have already been planted in a strip 4,500 kilometers long by 1,500 kilometers wide. The project aims to increase forest coverage to 23% of the total area of China in 2020. (La reforestation, 2018)

To meet the challenge, even the army was called upon in 2018: 60,000 soldiers were mobilized to reforest 84,000 square kilometers of arid land. (*ibid.*) According to a ranking by the United Nations Food and Agriculture Organization (FAO), the country that gained the most forest area between 2010 and 2015 was China. Also according to the FAO, about 13 million hectares of forests are lost each year in the world — the equivalent of a quarter of the surface area of France.

But there is a fly in the ointment for China's environmental policy: the country is now the largest furniture manufacturer in the world and it contributes actively to global deforestation with its imports of wood from many countries, especially from Southeast Asia and Africa. It was the top importer of industrial wood in 2019 and the second-largest importer of forest products.

China has at the same time become the world's largest manufacturer of photovoltaic panels. It needs to be. Beijing residents, for example, now live most of the time in thick smog that forces many to wear a mask, even when there is no global pandemic. China's big cities are choking due to air pollution caused by using coal for heating, with the

---

Tibet have fallen from 25.2 million hectares in 1950, when Tibet was invaded by the Chinese army, to 13.57 million hectares in 1985, due to the massive deforestation carried out by Chinese authorities in Tibet, which was traditionally the great reservoir of primary forests in Asia.

country being the biggest consumer of this fuel in the world. Poor air quality represents an average reduction in life expectancy of three and a half years for each Chinese man and woman, according to a study by the University of Chicago published in 2017. For residents of China's most polluted cities, the reduction in life expectancy is six and a half years. China shares with India the sad distinction of having the most polluted cities on the planet. The struggle against pollution has begun to make some progress, however. Air quality improved significantly in 2018 following a first improvement in 2017. In China's largest 338 cities the average level of fine particles 2.5 microns in diameter (PM 2.5) — which are very dangerous because they penetrate deep into the lungs — was 39 micrograms per cubic meter in 2018, a decrease of 9.3% from the previous year, according to a report from the Environment Ministry. In 2017, the concentration of these harmful particles had already decreased, but by a smaller proportion (−6.5%). The level remains well above the maximum threshold recommended by the World Health Organization (WHO) however, which is 10 micrograms per cubic meter. According to a study by the Chinese University of Hong Kong, air pollution represents a cost to the Chinese economy of 267 billion yuan ($40.7 billion) per year and is responsible for the premature deaths of over a million people. Beijing tightened the application of its environmental regulations in 2018, collecting a total of 15.28 billion yuan ($2.3 billion) in fines, a 32% increase over one year, according to a study by the Environment Ministry. Damage due to pollution, the hidden face of China's development, cost it between 6% and 9% of GDP each year over the period 1995–2005. (Huchet, 2016)

China also emits more than 200 million cubic meters of waste directly into the sea each year — the vast majority of it plastics — according to the Environment Ministry. (Xu & Stanway, 2019) The Chinese government reacted by announcing in January 2020 a ban on single-use plastic bags in major cities by the end of 2020 and throughout the rest of the country by 2022.

For the past decade, China has seemed more eager to meet its international environmental obligations. Beijing signed the Paris Agreement in December 2015.[2] The National People's Assembly ratified it in September 2016. China is one of the countries most exposed to the consequences of climate change. According to some international analyses, a rise in sea level linked to global warming could cause catastrophic flooding and massive economic losses in the Pearl River and Yellow River deltas. Hong Kong and Guangzhou could be partially submerged.

But not much has changed in practice in China since 2015. It remains by far the top country in terms of CO_2 emissions, ahead of the United States and India. At a UN climate summit in New York in September 2019, 66 countries set a target of achieving carbon neutrality by 2050, but China preferred to stay on the sidelines. Thirty countries have now joined an alliance promising to stop the construction of coal-fired power stations from 2020. The number of such plants under construction is declining all over the world, except in China, where capacity will increase another 30% by 2030. With nearly 1,000 gigawatts (GW), China alone holds almost half the worldwide capacity of coal-fired power plants, followed by the United States at 259 GW and India at 221 GW. Among these plants, many are "illegal", but they are rarely shut down. According to the American NGO Global Energy Monitor, China built enough new coal plants between January 2018 and June 2019 to reverse the efforts made in recent years in the rest of the world to reduce coal energy. (Shearer, Yu & Nace, 2019) Moreover, many coal-fired power stations are still being built abroad by Chinese companies. In 2018, Beijing invested $36 billion in power plants built by Chinese companies in developing countries. Chinese CO_2 emissions have increased 4.5-fold between 1990 and 2017. In 2017, China still accounted for 29% of global CO_2 emissions, more than double the level of US.

Xi Jinping delivered a veritable climate policy bombshell when he announced in his speech to the UN General Assembly on

---

[2] This agreement aims to limit global warming to +2°C by the end of the 21st century. 195 countries have signed it, but the United States announced its withdrawal on June 1, 2017.

September 22, 2020, that China would strive to achieve carbon neutrality by 2060. It is an ambitious objective, especially when combined with the pledge to reach peak CO_2 emissions "before 2030" instead of "around 2030" as indicated in its previous climate plan. Analysts view the declaration as being aimed for foreign public opinion, with China wishing to present itself as being responsible on the issue of climate change and draw a distinction with the United States' Donald Trump, who pulled the country out of the Paris Agreement and refused to enter any environmental pacts. But with coal still generating around 60% of the country's electricity and natural gas most of the rest, China has a long way to go.

Public debt is another threat hanging over the Chinese economy. A veritable time bomb, it now accounts for 15% of global debt, according to the Institute of International Finance. It has exploded in recent years, quadrupling between 2008 and 2016, to reach $28.4 trillion. In 2018, China's debt including household and non-financial companies, represented nearly 235% of national GDP, and 255% in the first quarter of 2019. So is China a giant with feet of clay? The IMF sounded the alarm bell in a 2019 report that warned China's debt may exceed 290% of its GDP by 2022. (IMF, 2019) According to the latest figures by the Institute of International Finance, it nearly reached 290% in the first quarter of 2020. For the IMF, an increase to such levels is dangerous as it will not leave much room for Chinese authorities to respond to potential economic shocks, and in particular to any acute problem in the inter-bank market or to a crisis of confidence in wealth management products which have fueled strong growth in the opaque banking sector. The number of companies defaulting on bonds has been rising. They quadrupled in 2018 to hit 122 billion yuan. In 2019 the figure rose to 130 billion yuan and credit ratings agency S&P Global Ratings has said it expects corporate defaults to increase again in 2020.[3] Between 2007 and 2017, the ratio of corporate debt vs GDP in China has climbed from 101% to 160%, according to Bloomberg News.

---

[3] https://www.spglobal.com/marketintelligence/en/news-insights/trending/RqEWG6 BuUZ0RPiJ1-q9CeA2

(Why China's debt defaults, 2019) If companies are unable to refinance their debt, there is the potential for considerable disruption to the economy.

Capital flight, which was already considerable in 2012, has accelerated since 2015, reflecting Chinese investors' lack of confidence in their economy. Some $1 trillion left China in 2015 and such massive outflows have continued since. Despite strict exchange controls implemented by the authorities, capital flight still reached an estimated $87.8 billion in the first quarter of 2019.[4] Since 2012, Chinese nationals have been allowed to leave the country with no more than $50,000 per person per year. Meanwhile, companies are only allowed to move money abroad as part of duly approved investment projects. But many possibilities exist to move money illegally, in particular via parallel banking institutions that get it to Hong Kong, where Chinese companies and rich individuals prefer to channel their wealth.

Over the past 20 years, a monstrous real estate bubble has grown in China which now constitutes a threat to its economic equilibrium. A frenzy of construction in the 1990s changed the face of China's cities. Billions of cubic meters of concrete were poured to raise millions of graceless buildings that now disfigure urban areas. When I was stationed in Beijing during the 1980s, the city presented the endearing face of a peaceful capital with its *hutongs*, its old traditional alleys where children played and old people lapped up the rays of the sun on chairs in front of the entrances to their *siheyuans*, their houses with square courtyards that Beijing was famous for. It was a real delight to stroll among them and discover the unexpected charms of a city where, all in all, life was good. Accompanying such a walk would be the trill of bicycle bells. But in today's Beijing, millions of bicycles have been replaced by millions of cars. The sun hardly shines anymore in a megalopolis hidden in smog most of the year. The *hutongs* and *siheyuans* have almost all been destroyed, with only a few spared to satisfy tourists. The residents were forcibly evicted by the police. The more

---

[4] Reuters, September 11, 2019.

fortunate were relocated to building complexes located on the distant outskirts of the city.

The urban land thus freed up triggered a wave of construction and speculation that sucked in nearly everyone in the country. Speculation pushed prices up to artificially high levels. The result was too many apartments were built. Tens of millions stand empty, including some entire buildings. Some 22% of the building stock is unoccupied, i.e. more than 50 million homes. Home buyers are heavily in debt, having been encouraged to borrow with easy mortgage terms. The stock of mortgage debt jumped by a factor of seven between 2008 and 2017, rising from 3 trillion yuan to the staggering sum of 22.9 trillion yuan ($3.3 trillion at the average 2017 exchange rate), according to figures from the People's Bank of China (PBOC), the central bank. Mortgage debt represented more than half of the total debt of Chinese households, which stood at 46.2 trillion yuan. (Le «scénario cauchemardesque», 2018) Household debt, as a percentage of income, has also risen sharply in recent years, from around 80% at the end of 2014 to nearly 130% at the end of 2019. For comparison, that was the level of debt to income US households had just before the market for mortgage-backed securities seized up in 2007, triggering the Great Recession. The US figure has since been trending back towards 100%. (Wright & Feng, 2020)

Real estate and construction currently represent about 15% of Chinese GDP. Already in 2016, Wang Jianlin, the boss of the Wanda[5] conglomerate, did not hide his concerns that the market had become uncontrollable in the face of the appetite of Chinese savers for property, which had been more profitable than the stock market and collecting interest on banking deposits. It's the "biggest bubble in history," Wang, who himself started out in commercial real estate, told CNNMoney in an interview. "I don't see a good solution to this problem," he said. "The government has come up with all sorts of measures — limiting purchase or credit — but none have worked". (Mullen & Stevens,

---

[5] Chinese conglomerate grouping together activities linked to tourism, hospitality and cinema.

2016) It remains another time bomb ticking away for the authorities. This cocktail of real estate fever and a surge in lending has similarities to America's subprime crisis, which triggered the global financial crisis in the late 2000s. In Shenzhen, up to 30% of real estate purchases were speculative investments, according to Xinhua news agency. What will happen when the bubble bursts?

Meanwhile, the spectacular progress of the private sector and its growing influence on Chinese society have led the authorities to gradually impose political barriers on its development in recent years. Private giants are indeed beginning to overshadow the Party and become key players in social life. There is a persistent rumor that Jack Ma was forced into early retirement as head of e-commerce giant Alibaba in September 2019 at the young age of 55 following the intervention of the Party. Jack Ma, like other big Chinese bosses and billionaires, had become an icon in China over the years. It was clear that if free elections were held in the country, Ma would far outscore Party leaders. "The pressure that the state has exerted on private enterprises is getting more and more evident. That includes policies requiring companies to set up (Communist) party committees or business executives to join the party" to name a few, said Emmy Hu, former editor-in-chief of Global e-Businessmen, a media platform created by Alibaba. (Huang, 2019)

Dismal demographics is now another serious hindrance to China's development. Because of the one-child policy introduced in 1979 by Deng Xiaoping, China's birth rate fell in 2018 for the first time since 1961, and that came about despite the ending of this policy in 2015. China's population also decreased in 2018, the first time that has happened in at least seventy years, dropping by 1.27 million people out of a total population of 1.39 billion. In 2019, there were only 14.65 million births in China, the lowest total since 1949, with the exception of 1961, a year marked by famine. This phenomenon is linked to factors such as the costs of raising and educating a child, which are very high in large cities, as well as the fear among women that having a child will harm their careers. Just as in rich countries, Chinese couples no longer want to have many children. One result is that the percentage of seniors in the population is increasing sharply. Another is that "in 2030, the number of women of childbearing age will have fallen by 31% compared to 2017. The number of births will fall to 11 million, a third less than in 2017," economist Ren Zeping noted in a January 2019 report published on the Chinese portal Sina. (Zhang, 2019) The fall is rapid and dizzying: by 2030 nearly 30% of people in China will be over 60 and by 2050 this will rise to 35.9%. China is set to lose its place as the most populous country in the world in 2027 to India, according to a UN report released in June 2019. The aging of the population also poses a problem for China's state coffers and the fragile pension system. According to 2016 figures from the finance ministry, pension spending rose 11.6% to 2,580 billion yuan ($388 billion at the average 2016 exchange rate). Without reform, the deficit of 600 billion yuan recorded in 2018 is expected to rise to 890 billion yuan in 2020, warned Wang Dehua, a researcher at the National Academy of Economic Strategy in Beijing, for whom China's greatest fiscal threat is the "retirement" risk. That fear is shared by Liu Shangxi, director of the Academy of Fiscal Sciences, who sees the deficit increasing "rapidly" after 2020. (De Maeyer, 2018) China has completely abandoned its birth control policy. The new Civil Code, which was adopted in May 2020, did not make any reference to controlling births. Meanwhile, the aging of the population is already pushing bosses to relocate to other countries as Chinese factories are starting to lack workers!

Even if President Xi Jinping remains popular, China's social stability is not as solid as it initially seems to be. Some 150,000 "social incidents" are recorded across the country each year, most often caused by land confiscations deemed to have been illegal, destruction of homes or neighborhoods, serious incidents of river pollution, labor disputes or conflicts with local governments that can often bring together several thousand demonstrators. Usually, the protesters avoid attacking local Party leaders directly. Higher-level authorities are usually able to find a solution, often by making local leaders the scapegoat. The Ministry of State Security, which is responsible for monitoring the population and which controls the police, is endowed with a huge budget that reached 1,390 billion yuan in 2018 ($199 billion at the average 2018 exchange rate) — much more than the money spent on the military. In January

2019, Xi Jinping mentioned for the first time the risk of a "black swan event", a low-probability event that triggers catastrophic consequences. Xi urged the authorities to remain "vigilant" against threats to the Party's political and ideological security in the context of a worrying economic slowdown. The government should focus on training programs among the younger generation to counter the influence of the internet and ensure the survival of "socialism with Chinese characteristics". "Now, the main front of the ideological struggle is on the internet, and the main audience of the internet is young people," Xi said. "Many domestic and foreign forces are trying to develop supporters of their values and even to cultivate opponents of the government" he added. (Brennan, 2019)

A "black swan" event did occur during the winter of 2019–2020 with the COVID-19 pandemic that originated in China's Wuhan region. While the regime has been more transparent than during the SARS outbreak in 2003, when the authorities attempted to cover up the epidemic, the local government in Wuhan and the central authorities lost precious time by maintaining a culpable silence for more than three weeks between the end of December 2019 and early January 2020, before being forced to reveal the extent of the outbreak and take drastic containment measures. The COVID-19 pandemic has cost China dearly, harming its public image as well as economic growth. But as China was the first to feel the economic shock of lockdowns meant to slow the spread of the novel coronavirus, it was also the first to recover. China's GDP rose by 3.2% in the second quarter of 2020 compared to the same quarter in 2019, a sign that the economy is getting back up to speed after a massive 6.8% drop in the first quarter. The Chinese economy grew by 11.5% in the second quarter from the first, according to official figures, thus avoiding a recession. In the third quarter GDP growth accelerated to 4.9% on an annual comparison, which meant China was the only major economy in the world to grow in 2020. Earlier in the year the IMF forecast that the Chinese economy would expand by 1% compared to an 8% drop for advanced economies. The growth rate is of course far from the 6.1% expansion China posted in 2019, which was already the lowest rate since China's economic boom began under Deng Xiaoping. And in another sign of the new times, the Chinese government has not set an annual growth target, a first in four decades.

While it is too early to draw all the necessary conclusions from the handling of the pandemic, it has certainly brought to light the shortcomings and weaknesses of a very rigid political pyramid structure where the lower echelons of power live in constant fear of swift punishment in the event that any initiative they take is deemed unwelcome. Hence the first COVID-19 whistleblower, Wuhan Central Hospital ophthalmologist Li Wenliang was served by police with a stern warning, which he had to sign, for "dissemination of false rumors which have seriously affected public order" when he revealed, on December 30, the existence of patients infected with an unknown virus related to SARS. Li, who was already infected with COVID-19, became a national hero after his death on February 6. His treatment by the authorities immediately sparked outrage and anger against the government on social networks, a phenomenon not seen for a long time in the country. "The truth will always be treated like a rumor. How long are you going to continue lying to us? Are you still lying? What are you still hiding?" wrote one user on Weibo, the popular social media site. "Don't forget how you feel now. Remember this anger. We can't allow this to happen again," said another. These messages, like many others, were quickly deleted by the censors. After February 6, hundreds of Chinese, including leading academics, signed an online petition calling for "freedom of expression". But the chances of seeing the authorities act on it are almost nil.

Like it or not, Xi Jinping seems to continue to have considerable public backing. In a country where public opinion polls are prohibited it is difficult to have a precise reading of sentiment, but according to the Edelman Trust Barometer 2020, the Chinese government benefits from one of the highest levels of public support in the world. On the other hand, the United States is in the bottom third of the 26 countries surveyed. Meanwhile, the results of a 10-year survey published by Harvard University researchers in July 2020 found that "since the start of the survey in 2003, Chinese citizen satisfaction with government has increased virtually across the board." (Cunningham, Saich & Turiel, 2020) In 2016, satisfaction with the Chinese central government reached 93%, a remarkable figure given that US presidents have not been able to garner favorable ratings much higher than 60%.

Finally, the last obstacle to China's development is corruption. It is an endemic evil that gnaws at all levels of the Party apparatus. Corruption has fed off the country's spectacular economic growth, which has provided ample opportunities for easy enrichment to the cadres of the CCP and the "red princes", these sons of Communist dignitaries who have become successful through their *guanxi* (connections). Xi Jinping achieved some popularity when he started an all-out war on corruption shortly after coming to power. He targeted all levels of power: the "tigers" and the "flies" among Party officials, government figures, soldiers, heads of state companies. In a big first in China, he succeeded in bringing down a member of the CPC Politburo Standing Committee, the powerful former head of the public security ministry Zhou Yongkang, who was sentenced in 2015 to life imprisonment for taking bribes, abuse of power and disclosure of state secrets. The following year, Zhou's wife and son were in turn sentenced to nine and eighteen years in prison. The prosecution of the Zhous, widely commented on by the official press, made a deep impression on public opinion and led many to think that the big "tigers" of the regime were no longer untouchable. Shortly after the fall of Zhou Yongkang followed that of one of his political allies, Bo Xilai, son of a senior CCP dignitary and general secretary of the giant municipality of Chongqing in southwestern China. His sentencing to life imprisonment in a landmark trial demonstrated Xi Jinping's determination to do away with a profound evil that angers ordinary Chinese people and above all raises doubts about the future of the system. In total, 1.5 million party cadres have been dismissed from their posts and punished since 2013, according to estimates by Western observers. The purge has not stopped, but it had two almost immediate consequences. On the one hand, Xi Jinping created strong enmities within the Party with which he must now reckon. On the other hand, corrupt cadres have mostly taken a step back from their activities, hoping to go undiscovered and waiting for a return of better days. But in fact, "corruption is so deeply rooted in the nature of the regime that it will never disappear," says a well-informed Chinese source in Hong Kong who considers that the level of corruption in China has risen so high that it threatens the survival of the regime. China was ranked very low on the Corruption Perceptions Index (CPI) compiled by the German NGO Transparency International in 2018. The survey ranked China in 87th place out of 180 countries, putting it below India, which came in at 78th place.

Can China continue to keep democracy at arm's length as it opens to an outside world full of new digital technologies? China is innovating to turn these technologies to its purpose, pioneering the use of a massive surveillance and social rating system for its population. And while Chinese censors may exercise very tight control over information in the country, the Chinese are well aware of what is happening in the rest of the world. Is democracy foreign to the Confucian thought that inspires the Chinese leadership? According to the French historian of contemporary China, Pierre-Étienne Will, China can look to its own democratic past. The Confucian philosopher Mencius more than two thousand years ago developed the notion of the primacy of the people over the sovereign. The people were considered as the "foundation of the nation" and "that which is the most precious". He believed they had the right to rebel against a sovereign unworthy of his mission. Today, any whiff of aspirations for more democracy are systematically snuffed out. But for how long can this continue?

The massive demonstrations that have taken place in Hong Kong since March 2019, in addition to tarnishing the image of China on the international scene, reflect a powerful aspiration among the people of the former British colony for more freedom and democracy. On June 9, 2019, over one million Hong Kong residents demonstrated in the streets against the growing political influence of mainland China. On June 16, a veritable human tidal wave of more than 2 million demonstrators took to the streets. That is more than one in four inhabitants, even including senior citizens and babies. On January 1, 2020, more than a million protesters once again took to the streets. Faced with the scale of the protest, the central government, to everyone's surprise, backed down. Carrie Lam, Hong Kong's chief executive, announced on September 4 the withdrawal of a bill providing for the extradition of suspects to China, which would have sounded the death knell for the independence of local justice. But the protesters wanted more and among their demands was respect for their civil rights and the organization of elections using direct universal suffrage. These were requests that Beijing could not accept. This was the most serious crisis in Hong Kong since its transition to Chinese sovereignty in 1997. Beijing found itself in a dilemma as it was impossible to cede more to protesters due to the risk of a contagion effect on the mainland. But to send the army in to quell dissent would deal a terrible blow to the image of China and would mark the definitive end of Hong Kong's role as a financial hub, a function that is very important for Beijing. Yet letting the situation in Hong Kong fester came at a considerable cost for Beijing as it swung the presidential election in Taiwan in January 2020. Polls taken in early 2019 indicated Tsai Ing-wen was going to lose her reelection bid to her Kuomintang competitor, Han Kuo-yu, who was more accommodating to Beijing. But Han's stance became a liability as the year wore on while Tsai repeatedly expressed her support for protesters in Hong Kong, speaking of a "fight for freedom and democracy", and vociferously rejected the idea of reunification with the Chinese mainland. In the end she comfortably won reelection.

The Sino-British joint declaration signed in Beijing in September 1984 by Chinese Premier Zhao Ziyang and his British counterpart Margaret Thatcher, which came into force the following year, set the terms for Hong Kong's return to China. Beijing pledged to respect the capitalist system, civil liberties and the way of life in the former colony for fifty years, that is until 2047. This was all part of a special status for the territory, which Deng Xiaoping described as "one country, two systems". The same solution also applied to Macau after the return of the former Portuguese colony to Chinese sovereignty in 1999. It was also proposed, without success, to the people of Taiwan as a formula to complete the reunification with the Chinese "motherland", and this option is now politically moribund. Hong Kong, a "special administrative region" of China, has become a painful thorn in the side of the Chinese communist regime. In their classic manner, Chinese authorities denounce foreign interference in the unrest in Hong Kong, particularly from the United States but also the United Kingdom, the former colonial power. Hong Kong is a precious financial center for the Chinese regime. The amount of US treasury bills held by Chinese companies in the former British colony totaled $72.3 billion in 2018, out of a total of some $12 trillion in privately held US debt. Hong Kong is also a tax haven for Chinese elites, including the "red princes". Some $3.1 trillion in private funds passed through Hong Kong financial firms in 2018. Finally, 79% of global foreign exchange transactions denominated in renminbi (yuan) in 2018 transited through Hong Kong.

With the crisis still unresolved, Hong Kong entered recession in October 2019. At the start of the same month, during a stay in the city, I was able to observe the demonstrations. There were youths as young as 12–14 years old on the streets! It is an indication of just how desperate a fight the Chinese authorities have on their hands. On October 13, 2019, during an official visit to Nepal, Xi Jinping sent a stern warning to demonstrators. "Anyone attempting to split China in any part of the country will end in crushed bodies and shattered bones," Xi said. (Xi Jinping warns, 2019) In fact, the divide between the population of Hong Kong and China runs deep and scars will remain regardless of the outcome of the crisis. When police charge during protests and young protesters flee inside neighboring buildings, the inhabitants open their doors and offer them refuge. "China does not inspire. The best example is Hong Kong. There is no stronger challenge to China than on the fringes of the country, where we should, on the contrary, find people fascinated by their model," says Stéphanie Balme, a China specialist and professor at Sciences Po in Paris, where she heads up the Law, Justice and Society in China program. (Balme, 2019)

On November 24, 2019, candidates from the Hong Kong pro-democracy movement scored an overwhelming victory in the elections for district committees, winning 17 of 18 districts and 347 of 452 seats, a political tsunami which at the same time inflicted a humiliating setback on the pro-Beijing leaders of the former British colony.

The unprecedented participation rate of 71.2% out of nearly 3 million voters (many of whom had never voted previously in their lives), illustrated, if that was indeed necessary, the sentiment of Hong Kong people to what they perceived to be increasing Chinese interference in the territory. On the day of the elections, there were no demonstrations in the streets. Activists had called for calm to allow voting to take place without incident. District committees have very few real powers, being essentially responsible for the management of car parks, bus routes and garbage collection. But the elected councilors choose 117 from among themselves to sit on the 1,200-member Commission that selects Hong Kong's leadership. The pro-democracy activists now hold nearly half of the seats on the Commission. Admittedly, Beijing retains the final say on the selection of the executive leadership. On the Chinese mainland, the official media did report the elections, but without giving any results! On November 27, 2019, Donald Trump signed into law a measure approved a week earlier by an overwhelming majority of Congress, which expressed America's support for pro-democracy activists and threatened, due to the lack of respect for human rights, to suspend the special economic status granted by Washington to Hong Kong. Beijing called the legislation an "absolute abomination" and threatened the United States with "retaliatory action".

China eventually moved to tighten the screws on Hong Kong. On June 30, 2020, the government in Beijing adopted a national security law concerning the territory. The parliament approved it unanimously. After being signed by Xi Jinping it was incorporated into Hong Kong's Basic Law, which has since 1997 served as the territory's mini-constitution, and immediately went into effect. Under the law, anyone found guilty of "*separatism*", "*terrorism*", "*subversion*", or "*colluding with external or foreign forces*" risks a sentence that can be as severe as life imprisonment. The adoption of the law, which was clearly meant to snuff out opposition in the territory, spells the end of democratic liberties and no doubt also sounds the death knell for the "one nation, two systems" policy. "#Beijing has just passed the sweeping #nationalsecuritylaw. It marks the end of Hong Kong that the world knew before," prominent democracy activist Joshua Wong posted on his Twitter feed.

After overcoming its shock over the development, Britain expanded the opportunities for Hong Kong people to reside in the UK and eventually seek citizenship. The 2.9 million of them who hold British national (overseas) passports will be able to live, work and study in Britain for up to five years compared to six months previously. After the end of that period they gain the status of residents, and a year after that, they can request citizenship. Australia has also offered to take in Hong Kong residents. Meanwhile, Donald Trump announced the definitive end of the special economic status the US had granted Hong Kong.

For Jacques Gravereau, founder and director of the HEC Eurasia Institute, China will not be the hyperpower of the twenty-first century. Its demographic crisis, pace of technological innovation that still largely lags behind that of the United States, rampant corruption that stifles the Party and society, a cruel lack of *soft power*, and sustained isolation in the world all mean China cannot claim the top ranking in the world.

> The rest of the world will not line up behind doubtful Chinese values. Moreover, if China becomes the dominant world power, that will mean that the United States has agreed, voluntarily or not, to abdicate its superpower role both in reality and in perception and that its *soft power* has been lost. All of this is highly improbable. (Gravereau, 2017: 258, 259)

According to this Asia specialist, the United States will remain the world leader for some time to come yet. China "will undoubtedly be one of the very great powers of the twenty-first century. But not the hyperpower. The world order will not be Chinese," he concludes. (*ibid.*)

For Valérie Niquet, an expert on Asian strategic issues and a senior researcher at the Paris-based Foundation for Strategic Research (FRS), as long as China "has not overcome its handicaps, at the price probably of an accepted evolution if not a change of regime, it will not be able to impose itself as the superpower of the twenty-first century." (Niquet, 2017) In effect, she believes that "the role of the Communist Party, while acting as an accelerator, also weighs on the freedom to innovate" and "this refusal of political change had already shattered the reformist momentum that could have won out in the final years of the Empire, at the end of the 19th century. Today, it risks interrupting the ramp-up of a regime whose priority is to ensure its survival."[6]

Renaud Girard, a seasoned journalist and senior reporter at *Le Figaro*, is not far from sharing this opinion. China, he has said, will not be able to "subjugate its Asian neighbors" for ideological, geopolitical and economic reasons. "Politically, Xi Jinping's China is being perceived as a threat by its neighbors. They did not accept it forcibly grabbing the reefs and waters of the South China Sea," he wrote. (Girard, 2019)

For Graham Allison on the other hand, "nobody believes in communism any more in China. A party dominating society can successfully govern a stable and sustainable system... But the unfolding events in Hong Kong show that with its opening-up policy, the Chinese regime is exposing itself to mounting demands for more democracy." Chinese GDP, calculated in terms of purchasing power parity, already exceeds that of the United States by 20% and "China's economy could be twice the size of the US economy by 2025 and three times, or even four times the size of the US economy by 2040... Most Americans do not believe this scenario but it is a reality. I see this as a considerable systemic risk."[7]

Some Chinese intellectuals and foreign observers predict the imminent end of the Chinese Communist Party's reign and the collapse of the one-party system. Many believe that to be wishful thinking. But Minxin Pei, professor at Claremont McKenna College in California, is a believer.

After nearly 70 years in power, China's one-party regime is approaching the longevity frontier for dictatorship amid an economic slowdown and tensions with the US... A crackdown on opponents and an emphasis on nationalism may boost support in the short term but staying in power to celebrate the Party's centenary will be a challenge... the one-party regime may not even

---

[6] It should be noted that Huawei has sued Valérie Niquet for defamation after remarks she made in a February 2019 appearance on the French TV program *C dans l'air.*
[7] Interview with the author, September 16, 2019.

survive until 2049... The greatest threat to the Party's long-term survival lies in the unfolding cold war with the US... With its superior military capabilities, technology, economic efficiency, and alliance networks (which remain robust, despite President Donald Trump's destructive leadership), the US is far more likely to prevail in the Sino-American cold war than China. Though an American victory could be Pyrrhic, it would more than likely seal the Party's fate. (Pei, 2019)

For his part, the German sinologist Gunter Schubert, a researcher at the European Research Center on Contemporary Taiwan (ERCCT), believes that:

Economic development, social stratification, political decentralization, the rise of social movements, integration into the global market, the influence of the internet, and last but not least — the search by China for greater international respect, are factors to be taken into consideration since they contribute to the weakening of the authoritarian and one-party regime. (Schubert, 2003: 16)

Jean-Pierre Cabestan, a professor at Hong Kong Baptist University and a researcher at CNRS, remains cautious. The CCP, he stresses, is still firmly at the head of the country and it does not show any signs of an imminent collapse. "In many ways it is firmly at the controls. First, because there is repression which prevents any opposition from forming but also because most Chinese accept this state of affairs or, at the least, do not question it. Either they don't care about politics, or they think the Communist Party is the guarantor of stability and that a participatory democracy would wreak havoc in China. Many people in China believe in this argument. And also because they are nationalists and the Communist Party is the best defender of nationalism. The Chinese accept the Communist Party they inherited without questioning it too much. The main reason being the long-running, even ancient alienation of most Chinese people from politics.

So will the Party impose its law beyond 2049, the hundredth anniversary of the founding of the People's Republic of China? I bet it won't make it and will lose power before then. There are still forces of erosion. Until now the Party could claim credit for having developed China. This is something the

Chinese appreciate. There is a stability factor here. In the longer term, the Party dictatorship translates into a very repressive and very secretive regime. The population aspires to more information on the use of its taxes and on the way their country is run. With the emergence of a middle class which, in time, could represent half or more of the population, due to China's urbanization, there is a demand from the population which represents an erosion factor. China will want to evolve towards something else. A scenario of a radical change in the nature of the regime is likely 20 to 30 years from now."[8]

Chinese researcher and journalist Willy Wo-lap Lam, a professor at the Center for China Studies at the Chinese University of Hong Kong, emphasizes for his part that the Chinese people are traditionally very resilient. "The Chinese are not rebels. They are happy with their destiny. If they are not happy, they migrate to Australia, Canada or the United States," he says. Since 1949, the Communist Party has imposed "a perfect dictatorship" which is perpetuated "thanks to round-the-clock police surveillance with the help of artificial intelligence and hundreds of millions of spy cameras. This system is very efficient, China is the world champion for the number of its surveillance cameras. But the Party is obliged to realize today that it does not have legitimacy based on the ballot box," he explains. The current economic slowdown has hit the lower class hard, while the wealthy have been relatively spared. "No miracle can last forever. The Chinese miracle actually ended when Xi Jinping arrived in power. Growth fell back to 6.2%, but independent economists in Beijing do not believe this figure and are of the opinion that the real growth rate is more likely around 2% or 3%. That is where the problem is. For the lower class, growth this low signifies a virtual stagnation in their standard of living."[9]

For David Shambaugh, director of the China Policy Program at the Elliott School of International Affairs at George Washington University in Washington DC, "there has been a fundamental sea change, in my

---

[8] Interview with the author, October 5, 2019.
[9] Interview with the author, October 4, 2019.

view, in the way the US deals with China" and this change did not "happen overnight, it did not happen as a result of Trump." (Shambaugh, 2019)

I would argue even though cooperation [was the norm] competition has always kind of co-existed in the US-China relationship. The cooperative element had long been the dominant element and the competitive element was secondary. Now that's flipped and the competitive element is by far predominant... And I have used the word competition. I am not talking about containment. I am not talking about confrontation... Competition is exactly that — you compete for primacy, you compete for influence, you compete for position, you compete for allies and partners... As far as I am concerned [this competition will last] indefinitely, for a very long time. It is the single most important factor in international relations in our lifetimes and many other things will be affected by that and other nations are going to be caught increasingly in this competition and in some regions such as Southeast Asia they are really feeling the heat and feeling the pressure... to choose between the US and China... Now if the United States is wise in this competition it will not force other countries into such a choice. (Shambaugh, 2019)

Shambaugh compared the situation to a sports match with no end and no referees. The game constantly ebbs and flows. Each side scores tactical victories and suffers some setbacks. But with no final outcome to the contest.

So this is going to be very protracted and we'll kind of go on in this sort of low or medium intensity boil unless there is a trigger incident in the military domain, an accident in the South China Sea or elsewhere that could escalate into a more kinetic exchange between the two powers. I don't anticipate that. I certainly don't want that. (*Ibid.*)

David Zweig, emeritus professor of social sciences at Hong Kong University, also predicts a long period of cold war between the United States and China, but emphasizes that a decline of the United States should not be expected. "America can stay ahead. Not long ago, people started thinking America was finished. But it has shown a vibrancy to come back...," Zweig said in an interview. And while

China is rising rapidly, he believes it has a long way to go and notes that the United States is not standing still. "So maybe thirty, forty, fifty years from now the Chinese may catch up, but again that's a long time. There are a lot of black swan events that can happen and China's leadership screw up."

Zweig also believes it is wrong to anticipate the imminent demise of the current political system in China. Chinese leaders over the past forty years have "overcome pretty serious problems. Huge deficits, the global financial crisis, East Asia's financial crisis, Tiananmen square, Trump, so far they are doing okay and through all this, the Party is still quite strong, probably pretty popular... They are one of the most popular governments in Asia. People fail to recognize that. We may not like them, we don't like what they do here in Hong Kong... But there is a difference between your philosophy and what you see."

He recognized that a serious slowdown in the economy would make it harder for the Party to survive. "But as long as they can continue some kind of economic growth, where people feel that tomorrow is at least as good as today and maybe even a little better, they are okay."[10]

For Jean-Philippe Béja, sinologist and emeritus research director at CNRS-CERI-Sciences-Po, Xi Jinping's crackdown on emerging civil society and strengthening of the Party leadership after coming to power eliminated certain freedoms and established a cult of personality. Given party hegemony over society and government, a leadership cult, and nationalism, he believes that China can't even be considered a dictatorship hiding behind the trappings of democracy. Rather he sees it as a fully-fledged dictatorship that more and more resembles fascism:

> The Chinese Communist Party (CCP) has not changed since 1989. The rapid development of the economy did not translate into democratization. On the contrary, the embryo of civil society that appeared at the turn of the century has been repressed. In July 2015, police arrested more than 300 human rights

---

[10] Interview with the author, October 17, 2019.

defense lawyers and 20 of them were sentenced to prison terms following humiliating self-criticism sessions broadcast on television. (Beja, 2019)

China "will one day have to resolve the fundamental contradiction between its economic and cultural openness to the world and its increased desire to control individuals, organizations and ideas," says Asia specialist Hubert Testard. (Testard, 2019b)

Conclusion

Just when America seems to have both lost its steam and its way, China has achieved a multifaceted breakthrough unique in the world. What will emerge from the clash between these two great adversaries? Already, China's expansionism is provoking growing mistrust among its partners, as well as creating obstacles along its path. Meanwhile, Beijing appears to be approaching its long-term ambitions of conquest like a chess master, while US leaders make only short-term blocking moves. So, should we expect an armed conflict between China and the United States? In all likelihood, no. At least not for the foreseeable future. China needs a peaceful environment to continue its development and rise on the world stage. According to Jean-Pierre Cabestan:

> For the People's Republic, economic development, social stability and the survival of the one-party political regime remain and will remain priorities. Another is to make China a very great power, but is competition with the United States for the top spot an overriding goal? Some Chinese believe it is, or they are willing to play this dangerous game. But the government is keeping a cool head, taking calculated risks and not venturing outside the gray areas it knows best how to exploit... it avoids getting caught in dangerous situations from which it cannot escape. In other words, China calculates its "shots" well. (Cabestan, 2018b)

President Donald Trump was the first Western leader to dare to challenge China's increasing power directly.[1] Will others follow his lead?

---

[1] Donald Trump is not quite the only one who dares to challenge China. In October 2019, the municipal council of the city of Prague decided to break its sister city

Europe has started to take a common stance against some of China's ambitions. In the medium term, all major research institutes agree that China will become the top economic power around 2030. But for how long? A falling birth rate, mounting internal pressures for greater democracy, slowing economic growth, rising production costs, the social and political repercussions of opening up to the outside world, corruption; these all stand in the way of China's continued rapid advance. The United States will remain the world's military superpower for many years to come but the ultimate result of the cold war between the two great nations remains uncertain. It is up to democracy to prove its strength and vitality in the struggle against dictatorship.

The vision of a future world that is emerging in China is frightening in many ways. The Chinese Communist Party presides over a vast obscurantist system of surveillance[2] and of one-track thinking, enforced by cutting-edge technology and accepted by much of the population. This stands in contrast with an American society shaped by individualism, fascinated by weapons and violence, which may sometimes be politically chaotic but which is free. Chinese nationalism is fed by justified pride in the ingenuity and effort that has won such enormous

---

agreement with Beijing to mark its disagreement with Chinese policy towards Tibet, Xinjiang and Taiwan. The Chinese embassy replied by urging the city of Prague to "recognize its mistakes and not to deviate from the course of history at the risk of harming its interests", remarks immediately condemned by Czech Foreign Minister Tomáš Petříček, for whom diplomacy is not made with threats.

[2] According to a study by the German company Cure 53 specializing in cybersecurity, commissioned by the Open Technology Fund, an organization funded by the United States, the Chinese authorities launched in February 2019 a "free" app dedicated to "Xi Jinping thought" for holders of smartphones equipped with Android software (80% of the smartphone market in China): the Xuexi qiangguo or "Study the Great Nation" app. This app, which was the most downloaded in China for months, ostensibly takes users to a game of questions and answers on the extent of their knowledge about their country and their leader Xi Jinping. But thanks to a backdoor, it allows the authorities to spy on all the activities on a user's phone (emails, photos, messages, contacts, browsing history). The 90 million CCP members and government officials have been instructed to use it almost every day. (Washington Post, October 14, 2019)

economic success. But should the world turn a blind eye to the violent imposition of Han Chinese culture and communist values on the people of Xinjiang and Tibet, to the repression of democrats in Hong Kong and the denial of important freedoms to the Chinese people themselves?

Should the rest of the world continue to view China's economic triumph chiefly as a massive business opportunity or might it begin to question whether indebtedness to Beijing and reliance on Chinese manufactures bring unacceptable risks. China's rapid emergence as a serious military force in its own immediate region and beyond lends added urgency to these questions.

The Chinese Communist Party no longer seeks, as it once did, to export its ideology. At a time when the great Western idea of democracy is being undermined by the rise of populism in France, Italy, the United Kingdom, in Eastern Europe countries, in Brazil and elsewhere, roles appear curiously reversed today. While Donald Trump regularly championed protectionism, patriotism and unilateralism, Xi Jinping praises the virtues of multilateralism and globalism, as he did at the Davos Economic Forum in January 2017.

The danger lies in the nationalism which China's current leadership so often calls on when addressing its domestic audience and which its "Wolf Warrior" diplomats now demonstrate abroad.

On October 1, 2019, Xi Jinping exchanged his customary Western business suit for a dark Mao costume and stood on the Gate of Heavenly Peace in Beijing, from which Mao Zedong, exactly 70 years before, had proclaimed the founding of the People's Republic of China. That distant event offered hope the long-suffering country would have progress, prosperity and reclaim its rightful place in the world.

Mao instead drove China into further decades of misery until, after 1979, his eventual successor Deng Xiaoping confronted the impoverished country with the truth of its terrible backwardness, unleashing a patient process of economic growth from the ground up, of learning and of military modernization.

When Xi returned to the Tiananmen Gate for the momentous anniversary, heavy with symbolism, his clear message to the world, especially to the US administration, was that China had at long last arrived as a power to be reckoned with, respected or even feared.

"No force can stop the advance of the Chinese people," Xi proclaimed.

Such nationalist rhetoric aside, if the Chinese people are to have a lasting positive influence on the world, they must one day adopt democracy. In its rivalry with the United States, China relies on a totalitarian political model that belongs to the past and offers nothing to win over or inspire people outside its own borders.

By contrast, American democracy showed its robustness to the world with the presidential elections on November 3, 2020, that brought victory to Democrat Joe Biden despite the apparent efforts of the Republican populist incumbent, Donald Trump, to resort to his lawyers in a bid to cling to the White House after the vote went against him.

No one can predict for sure whether the Chinese Communist Party will last in power for another 10, 20 or 50 years, but one day China will join the march of history and give lie to those in the West who promote the absurd notion that democracy is not suited to the Chinese people.

Bibliography[1]

ABI-HABIB, Maria. 2018. China's Belt and Road Plan in Pakistan takes a military turn. *New York Times*. December 19. URL: https://www.nytimes.com/2018/12/19/world/asia/pakistan-china-belt-road-military.html

AFP. 2019. Fusion nucléaire: la Chine s'échauffe au soleil artificiel de demain. *Sciences et avenir*. 28 avril. URL: https://www.sciencesetavenir.fr/fondamental/fusion-nucleaire-la-chine-s-echauffe-au-soleil-artificiel_133304

ALLISON, Graham. 2019 [2017]. *L'Amérique et la Chine dans le piège de Thucydide ?* Vers la guerre. Paris: Odile Jacob.

AMALVY, Rémi. 2019. L'exploitation du deuxième EPR de la centrale chinoise de Taishan va débuter. *L'Usine nouvelle*. 7 septembre. URL: https://www.usinenouvelle.com/article/l-exploitation-du-deuxieme-epr-de-la-centrale-chinoise-de-taishan-va-debuter.N881755

Angela Merkel exhorte l'UE à adopter une stratégie commune vis-à-vis de la Chine. 2019. *Le Figaro*. 27 novembre. URL: https://www.lefigaro.fr/conjoncture/angela-merkel-exhorte-l-ue-a-adopter-une-strategie-commune-vis-a-vis-de-la-chine-20191127

A new study tracks the surge in Chinese loans to poor countries. 2019. *The Economist*. July 13. URL: https://www.economist.com/finance-and-economics/2019/07/13/a-new-study-tracks-the-surge-in-chinese-loans-to-poor-countries

ARZT, Richard. 2018. Le grand bond vers l'espace de la Chine. *Slate*. 14 octobre. URL: http://www.slate.fr/story/168470/chine-espace-programme-spatial-station-lunaire-cnsa

—— 2019. Chine et États-Unis, 75 ans de relations compliquées. *Slate*. 7 juin. URL: http://www.slate.fr/story/178089/etats-unis-chine-relations-75-ans-guerre-commerciale-donald-trump-xi-jinping

---

[1] The links were verified on November 1, 2020.

AXE, David. 2019a. Defense disaster: Russia and China are crushing the US military in war games. *The National Interest*. March 11. URL: https://nationalinterest.org/blog/buzz/defense-disaster-russia-and-china-are-crushing-us-military-war-games-46677

—— 2019b. China will soon have 3 aircraft carriers (with more to come). *National Interest*. October 30. URL: https://nationalinterest.org/blog/buzz/china-will-soon-have-3-aircraft-carriers-more-come-92121

BALME, Stéphanie. 2019. «Soft power», dur, dur, pour un régime autoritaire. *Pour l'éco*. hors série. octobre, p. 30.

BARRET, Philippe. 2018. *N'ayez pas peur de la Chine*. Paris: Robert Laffont.

BECKER, Jasper. 1996. *Hungry ghosts, Mao's secret famine*. London: Murray.

—— 2007. *Dragon rising: An inside look at China today*. Washington (DC): National Geographic.

BÉJA, Jean-Philippe. 2004. *À la recherche d'une ombre chinoise. Le mouvement pour la démocratie en Chine (1919–2004)*. Paris: Seuil.

—— 2019. La position de Xi Jinping n'est pas si confortable qu'elle en a l'air. *Le Monde*. 24 mars. URL: https://www.lemonde.fr/idees/article/2019/03/24/jean-philippe-beja-la-position-de-xi-jinping-n-est-pas-si-confortable-qu-elle-en-a-l-air_5440505_3232.html

BÉJA, Jean-Philippe, BONNIN, Michel, PEYRAUBE, Alain. 1991. *Le tremblement de terre de Pékin*. Paris: Gallimard.

BELL, Daniel. 2015. *The China model, political meritocracy and the limits of democracy*. Princeton: Princeton University Press.

BERGER, Annick. 2019. Les entreprises européennes sont elles menacées par le système de notation chinois ?. *Capital*. 25 septembre. URL: https://www.capital.fr/economie-politique/les-entreprises-europeennes-sont-elles-menacees-par-le-systeme-de-notation-chinois-1351208

BERGÈRE, Marie-Claire. 2013. *Chine, le nouveau capitalisme d'État*. Paris: Fayard.

BOISSEAU DU ROCHER, Sophie, DUBOIS DE PRISQUE, Emmanuel. 2019. *La Chine e(s)t le monde*. Paris: Odile Jacob.

BRADY, Anne-Marie. 2017. *China as a polar great power*. Cambridge: Cambridge University Press.

BONIFACE, Pascal, VÉDRINE, Hubert. 2019. *Atlas des crises et des conflits*. Paris: Armand Colin.

BONNIN, Michel. 2004. *Génération perdue, Le mouvement d'envoi des jeunes instruits à la campagne en Chine, 1968–1980*. Paris: EHESS.

BOUC, Alain. 1981. *Le libéralisme contre la démocratie: les procédés politiques du capitalisme libéral*. Paris: Le Sycomore.

BOUGON, François. 2017. *Dans la tête de Xi Jinping*. Arles: Actes Sud.

—— 2019. *La Chine sous contrôle.* Paris: Seuil.

BRENNAN, David. 2019. Xi Jiping: China facing political struggle amid Donald Trump's trade war and sluggish economic growth. *Newsweek.* January 22. URL: https://www.newsweek.com/xi-jinping-china-trade-war-donald-trump-economic-growth-political-ideological-1299665

BROWN, Kerry. 2017. *CEO, China: the rise of Xi Jinping.* London: I.B. Tauris.

BROWNE, Andy. 2019. Foothills of a Cold War. *Bloomberg.* November 21. URL: https://www.bloomberg.com/news/newsletters/2011/-foothills-of-a-cold-war

CABESTAN, Jean-Pierre. 2015. *La politique internationale de la Chine: Entre intégration et volonté de puissance.* Paris: Les Presses de Sciences Po.

—— 2018a. *Demain la Chine, démocratie ou dictature.* Paris: Gallimard.

—— 2018b. Le piège de Thucydide vu de Pékin; affirmer son leadership, éviter la guerre. *Le Débat,* n° 202/5, novembre-décembre, p. 14–15.

CARMONA, Yves, PHAM, Minh. 2019. Routes de la soie: à qui va le profit, la Chine ou les pays au bord de la route? *Asialyst.* 28 janvier. URL: https://asialyst.com/fr/2019/01/28/nouvelles-routes-de-la-soie-bri-chine-a-qui-va-profit/

CARROUÉ, Laurent. 2019. La Silicon Valley, un territoire productif au cœur de l'innovation mondiale et un levier de la puissance étatsunienne. *Géoconfluences.* 20 mai. URL: http://geoconfluences.ens-lyon.fr/informations-scientifiques/dossiers-regionaux/etats-unis-espaces-de-la-puissance-espaces-en-crises/articles-scientifiques/silicon-valley-territoire-productif-innovation

Ces experts militaires américains qui pensent que les États-Unis pourraient perdre une guerre avec la Chine. 2019. *Atlantico.* 29 juillet. URL: https://www.atlantico.fr/decryptage/3577019/ces-experts-militaires-americains-qui-pensent-que-les-etats-unis-pourraient-perdre-une-guerre-avec-la-chine-jean-bernard-pinatel-francois-gere

CHALIAND, Gérard, JAN, Michel. 2014. *Vers un nouvel ordre mondial.* Paris: Seuil.

CHAN, Tara F. 2019. State Department official on China threat: for first time US has 'great power competitor that is not Caucasian'. *Newsweek.* May 5. URL: https://www.newsweek.com/china-threat-state-department-race-caucasian-1413202

CHANG, Gordon. 2001. *The coming collapse of China.* New York: Random House.

CHEN, Yan. 2002. *L'éveil de la Chine.* La Tour d'Aigues: l'Aube.

CHENG, Anne. 2014. *Histoire de la pensée chinoise.* Paris: Seuil.

China is broadening its efforts to win over African audiences. 2018. *The Economist.* October 20. URL: https://www.economist.com/middle-east-and-africa/2018/10/20/china-is-broadening-its-efforts-to-win-over-african-audiences

China now has more diplomatic posts than any other country. 2019. *BBC.* November 27. URL: https://www.bbc.com/news/world-asia-china-50569237

China says has no intention to play 'Game of Thrones' but won't be threatened on trade. 2019 *Reuters*. September 12. URL: https://www.euronews.com/2019/09/25/chinas-wang-yi-rejects-us-criticisms-says-both-sides-should-cooperate

China-Russia joint exercise sends a message to Washington. 2019. *Agence France-Presse*. July 24. URL: https://www.rfi.fr/en/contenu/20190724-china-russia-joint-exercise-sends-message-washington

Chine: le nouvel aéroport Pékin-Daxing officiellement inauguré. 2019. *Air journal*. 25 septembre. URL: https://www.air-journal.fr/2015-chine-le-nouvel-aeroport-pekindaxing-officiellement-inaugure-5215189.html

Chine: les séparatistes seront «taillés en pièces». 2019. *Le Figaro*. 14 octobre. URL: https://www.lefigaro.fr/international/chine-les-separatistes-seront-tailles-en-pieces-20191014

Chinese diplomats must notify their moves in US. 2019. *BBC*. October 17. URL: https://www.bbc.com/news/world-asia-china-50078056

CHOL, Éric, FONTAINE, Gilles. 2019. *Il est midi à Pékin. Le monde à l'heure chinoise*. Paris: Fayard.

CLARK, Duncan. 2017. *Alibaba, L'incroyable histoire de Jack Ma, le milliardaire chinois*. Paris: Bourrin.

COCKER, Christopher. 2015. *The improbable war: China, the United States and the continuing logic of great power conflict*. New York: Oxford University Press.

COHEN, Claudia. 2019. La Chine interdit à 23 millions de « mauvais » citoyens de voyager. *Le Figaro*. 1er mars. URL: https://www.lefigaro.fr/conjoncture/2019/03/01/20002-20190301ARTFIG00319-la-chine-interdit-a-23-millions-de-citoyens-de-voyager-avec-son-systeme-de-credit-social.php

COURMONT, Barthélemy. 2019. La Chine, une obsession américaine. *Areion24*. 10 juin. URL: https://www.areion24.news/2019/06/10/la-chine-une-obsession-americaine/

CRÉDIT SUISSE. 2019. Global wealth report. October. URL: https://www.credit-suisse.com/about-us/en/reports-research/global-wealth-report.html

CROWSDTRIKE. 2019. Huge fan of your work: How turbine PANDA and China's top spies enabled Beijing to cut corners on the C919 passenger jet. October. URL: https://www.crowdstrike.com/blog/huge-fan-of-your-work-part-1/

CUFFE, James B. 2020. *China at a threshold, exploring social changing techno-social systems*. Abingdon: Routledge.

CUNNINGHAM, Edward, SAICH, Tony, TURIEL, Jessie. 2020. Understanding CCP resilience: Surveying Chinese public opinion through time. Ash Center for Democratic Governance and Innovation. URL: https://ash.harvard.edu/publications/understanding-ccp-resilience-surveying-chinese-public-opinion-through-time?utm_source=Ash%20Center%20for%20Democratic%20Governance%

20and%20Innovation&utm_campaign=1ebdcdbb3f-Weekly_email_37&utm_medium=email&utm_term=0_bc3d84c57d-1

DALL'ORSO, Laura. 2016. Chine et Pakistan, meilleurs amis de circonstance? *Portail de l'IE*. 27 janvier. URL: https://portail-ie.fr/analysis/1348/chine-et-pakistan-meilleurs-amis-de-circonstance

DELMAS-MARTY, Mireille, WILL, Pierre-Étienne. 2017. *La Chine et la démocratie*. Paris: Fayard.

DELURY, John. 2020. China as equal: Putting China as rival into historical context. *Perspectives on History*. American History Association. September 17. URL: https://www.historians.org/publications-and-directories/perspectives-on-history/october-2020/china-as-equal-putting-china-as-rival-into-historical-context

DE MAEYER, Paul. 2018. Démographie: l'inquiétant vieillissement de la Chine. *Aleteia*. 18 septembre. URL: https://fr.aleteia.org/2018/09/18/demographie-linquietant-vieillissement-de-la-chine/

DERON, Francis. 1989. *Cinquante jours de Pékin*. Paris: Christian Bourgois.

DOMENACH, Jean-Luc. 2008. *La Chine m'inquiète*. Paris: Perrin.

—— 1992. *Chine, l'archipel oublié*. Paris: Fayard.

—— 2002. *Où va la Chine?* Paris: Fayard.

—— 2007. *Comprendre la Chine d'aujourd'hui*. Paris: Perrin.

DUCHÂTEL, Mathieu, ZYLBERMAN, Boris. 2012. *Les nouveaux communistes chinois*. Paris: Armand Colin.

EBBERS, Haico A. 2019. *Unravelling modern China*. Singapore: World Scientific.

ECONOMY, Elizabeth C. 2019. *The third revolution: Xi Jinping and the new Chinese State*. New Delhi: Oxford University Press.

Egypt is a bit more ancient, Chinese President Xi tells Trump. 2017. *Agence France-Presse*. November 9. URL: https://english.alarabiya.net/en/variety/2017/11/09/Egypt-is-a-bit-more-ancient-Chinese-President-Xi-tells-Trump.html

EHRET, Ludovic, 2020. China successfully launches a Mars Rover Mission, joining the new space race. *Agence France-Presse*. July 23. URL: https://www.sciencealert.com/china-launches-a-mission-to-put-a-rover-on-mars-in-a-new-space-race

EKMAN, Alice. 2018. *La Chine dans le monde*. Paris: CNRS Editions.

ELMER, Keegan. 2019. US has woken up how 'truly hostile' China is towards Western values, says secretary of State Mike Pompeo. *South China Morning Post*. October 31. URL: https://www.scmp.com/news/china/diplomacy/article/3035707/us-has-woken-how-truly-hostile-china-towards-western-values

EMMOTT, Robin. 2019. In counterweight to China, EU, Japan sign deal to link Asia. *Reuters*. September 27. URL: https://www.reuters.com/article/us-eu-japan/in-counterweight-to-china-eu-japan-sign-deal-to-link-asia-idUSKBN1WC0U3

En Chine, votre visage suffit pour payer vos courses. 2019. *L'Expansion/AFP.* 4 septembre. URL: https://lexpansion.lexpress.fr/high-tech/video-en-chine-votre-visage-suffit-pour-payer-vos-courses_2096372.html

ESSLINGER, Olivier. 2019. L'ISS, la station spatiale internationale. *Astronomie et astrophysique.* mis à jour le 13 octobre. URL: https://www.astronomes.com/divers/liss-la-station-spatiale-internationale

ÉTIEMBLE, René. 1958. La Chine communiste devant son héritage culturel. *Politique étrangère,* 23/1, p. 48. URL: https://www.persee.fr/doc/polit_00342x_1958_num_23_1_2455

FALIGOT, Roger. 2015. *Les services secrets chinois de Mao à nos jours.* Paris: Nouveau Monde.

FENG, Gao. 2019. China unveils 'Patriotic Education' plan to include protest-hit Hong Kong. *Radio Free Asia.* November 14. URL: https://www.rfa.org/english/news/china/education-11142019145606.html

FISCHER, Joschka. 2012. China's Fifth Modernisation: Beijing needs a political transformation because it can only gain superpower status through cooperation, not coercion. *Gulf News.* April 26. URL: https://gulfnews.com/opinion/op-eds/chinas-fifth-modernisation-1.1013687.

FOUCART, Stéphane. 2019. Il est possible de nourrir la planète sans augmenter la surface cultivée. *Le Monde.* 8 août. URL: https://www.lemonde.fr/planete/article/2019/08/08/il-est-possible-de-nourrir-la-planete-sans-augmenter-la-surface-cultivee_5497701_3244.html

FRACHON, Alain, VERNET, Daniel. 2012. *La Chine contre l'Amérique, le duel du siècle.* Paris: Grasset.

FRANKOPAN, Peter. 2017. *Les routes de la soie.* Bruxelles: Nevicata.

—— 2019. *Les routes de la soie, L'histoire du cœur du monde.* Paris: Flammarion.

FRIEDBERG, Aaron L. 2011. *A contest for supremacy — China, America and the struggle for mastery in Asia.* New York: Norton & Company.

GADY, Franz-Stefan. 2019. F-35A Stealth Fighter Formally Enters Service in South Korea. *The Diplomat.* December 19. URL: https://thediplomat.com/2019/12/f-35a-stealth-fighter-formally-enters-service-in-south-korea/

GALACTÉROS, Caroline. 2019. Un nouveau partage du monde est en train de se structurer. *FigaroVox.* 9 novembre. URL: https://www.lefigaro.fr/vox/monde/caroline-galateros-un-nouveau-partage-du-monde-est-en-train-de-se-structurer-2019 1109

GEHRIGER, Urs. 2019. 'You can never be China's friend': Spengler. *Asia Times.* October 21. URL: https://www.asiatimes.com/2019/10/article/you-can-never-be-chinas-friend-spengler

GERNET, Jacques. 1972. *Le monde chinois.* Paris: Armand Colin.

GIRARD, Renaud. 2019. La Chine ne dominera jamais l'Asie. *Le Figaro.* 20 mai. URL: https://www.lefigaro.fr/vox/monde/renaud-girard-la-chine-ne-dominera-jamais-l-asie-20190520

GOHD, Chelsea, 2020. Russia has tested an anti-satellite weapon in space, US Space Command says. *Space.* July 23. URL: https://www.space.com/russia-tests-anti-satellite-weapon-in-space.html

GOLDMAN, David P. 2011. *How civilizations die.* Washington (DC): Regnery.

GOLUB, Philip. 2016. *East Asia's reemergence.* Cambridge: Polity Press.

—— 2019. Curbing China's rise. *Le Monde diplomatique.* Octobre. URL: https://mondediplo.com/2019/10/05china

GRAVEREAU, Jacques. 2017. *La Chine conquérante, enquête sur une étrange superpuissance.* Paris: Eyrolles.

GREEN, Tanner. 2018. Taiwan can win a war with China. Foreign Policy. September 25. URL: https://foreignpolicy.com/2018/09/25/taiwan-can-win-a-war-with-china/

GROUSSET, René. 2017. Histoire de la Chine, des origines à la Seconde Guerre mondiale. Paris: Payot.

Guerre commerciale Chine USA: les terres rares au cœur du conflit. 2019. *Euronews.* 16 août. URL: https://fr.euronews.com/2019/08/16/guerre-commerciale-chine-usa-les-terres-rares-au-c-ur-du-conflit

Guerre commerciale: Donald Trump annonce la reprise des négociations avec Pékin. 2019. *L'Opinion.* 26 août. URL: https://www.lopinion.fr/edition/international/guerre-commerciale-donald-trump-annonce-reprise-negociations-pekin-195700

Guerre des étoiles: Donald Trump lance un commandement de l'espace. 2019. *L'Express.* 30 août. URL: https://www.lexpress.fr/actualite/monde/amerique-nord/guerre-des-etoiles-donald-trump-lance-un-commandement-de-l-espace_2095974.html

GUIBERT, Nathalie. 2019. Les États-Unis et la Chine lancent une nouvelle guerre froide. *Le Monde.* 7 juin. URL: https://www.lemonde.fr/international/article/2019/06/02/les-etats-unis-et-la-chine-installent-une-nouvelle-guerrefroide_5470523_3210.html

GUILLAIN, Robert. 1966. Dans trente ans, La Chine. Paris: Seuil.

—— 1986. *Orient extrême, une vie en Asie.* Paris: Seuil.

GUILLERMAZ, Jacques. 1989. *Une vie pour la Chine, mémoires 1937–1989.* Paris: Robert Laffont.

—— 2004. *Le parti communiste chinois au pouvoir.* Préface de Michel Jan. Paris: Payot.

HARBULOT, Christian. 2017. *Le nationalisme économique américain.* Versailles: VA.

HOLSLAG, Jonathan. 2015. *China's coming war with Asia.* Cambridge: Polity Press.

—— 2019. Chine-États-Unis: «Comment une question commerciale est devenue une question de sécurité». *Le Monde.* 31 mai.

HOLZMAN, Marie, DEBORD, Bernard. 2005. *Wei Jingsheng, un Chinois inflexible.* Paris: Bleu de Chine.

HOLZMAN, Marie, MAMÈRE, Noël. 2009. *Chine, on ne bâillonne pas la lumière.* Paris: Jean-Claude Gawsewitch.

HOROWITZ Juliana Menasce, Ruth IGIELNIK and Rakesh KOCHHAR. 2020. Most Americans say there is too much economic inequality in the U.S., but fewer than half call it a top priority. *Pew Research Center.* January. URL: https://www.pewsocialtrends.org/2020/01/09/trends-in-income-and-wealth-inequality/

HOWIE, Fraser. 2012. *Red capitalism: The fragile financial foundation of China's extraordinary rise.* Singapore: Wiley & Sons.

HU, Ping. 2005. *Chine, à quand la démocratie?* Trad. par Marie Holzman. La Tour d'Aigues: l'Aube.

HUANG, Joyce. 2019. Have retired Jack Ma, Alibaba steered away from China communist party's clutches? *Voice of America.* September 18. URL: https://www.voanews.com/east-asia-pacific/have-retired-jack-ma-alibaba-steered-away-china-communist-partys-clutches

HUANG, Kristin. 2019. Sihanoukville's big gamble: The sleepy beach town in Cambodia that bet its future on Chinese money. *South China Morning Post.* September 24. URL: https://www.scmp.com/news/china/diplomacy/article/3025262/sihanoukvilles-big-gamble-sleepy-beach-town-bet-its-future

HUCHET, Jean-François. 2016. *La crise environnementale en Chine. Évolutions et limites des politiques publiques.* Paris: Presses de Sciences Po.

HUNTINGTON, Samuel. 1997. *Le choc des civilisations.* Paris: Odile Jacob.

HURT, Emma. 2019. President Trump called former president Carter to talk about China. *Wabe.* April 14. URL: https://www.wabe.org/president-trump-calls-president-carter-to-talk-china

HURUN RESEARCH INSTITUTE. 2019a. Lexus Hurun China rich list. Shanghai. October 10. URL: https://www.hurun.net/EN/Article/Details?num=CE08472BB47D

—— 2019b. Hurun global unicorn list 2019. October 21. URL: https://www.hurun.net/EN/Article/Details?num=A38B8285034B

IMF. 2019. People's Republic of China. Report n° 19/266. August 9. URL:https://www.imf.org/en/Publications/CR/Issues/2019/08/08/Peoples-Republic-of-China-2019-Article-IV-Consultation-Press-Release-Staff-Report-Staff-48576

IZAMBARD, Antoine. 2019. *France-Chine, les liaisons dangereuses.* Paris: Stock.

JACQUES, Martin. 2012. *When China rules the world: The rise of the Middle Kingdom and the end of the Western World.* London: Penguin Books.

JAN, Michel. 2003. *La Grande Muraille de Chine.* Paris: Payot.

—— 2013. Chine: à propos du Rêve chinois de Xi Jinping. *Asie 21-Futuribles*, n° 6, mai.

—— 2014. *Vers un nouvel ordre du monde*. Paris: Seuil.

JIANG, Mable. 2019. Xi Jinping's speech at the 18th Collective Study of the Chinese political bureau. *Medium*. October 26. URL: https://medium.com/@mablejiang/xijinpings-speech-at-the-18th-collective-study-of-the-chinesepolitical-bureau-of-the-central-1219730677b2

KANDEL, Maya. 2018. *Les États-Unis et le monde*. Paris: Perrin.

KANG, Sunyu, OTTONE, Mike. 2019. Confucius Institute set to close in early 2020. *The Review*. October 8. URL: http://udreview.com/confucius-institute-set-to-close-in-early-2020

KECK, Zachary. 2014. US-China rivalry more dangerous than cold war? *The Diplomat*. January 28. URL: https://thediplomat.com/2014/01/us-china-rivalry-more-dangerous-than-cold-war/

KISSINGER, Henry. 2012. *On China*. New York: Penguin.

La Chine n'a pas l'intention de jouer à «Game of thrones» sur la scène internationale selon le MAE chinois. 2019. *Xinhuanet*. 25 septembre. URL: http://french.xinhuanet.com/2019/25/c_138421923.htm

La reforestation de la Chine, le plus grand projet écologique au monde. 2018. *Green Innovation*. 14 décembre. URL: https://www.green-innovation.fr/2018/12/14/la-reforestation-de-la-chine-le-plus-grand-projet-ecologique-au-monde/

LAGUE, David. 2020. Special Report: U.S. rearms to nullify China's missile supremacy. *Reuters*. May 6. URL: https://www.reuters.com/article/us-usa-china-missiles-specialreport/special-report-u-s-rearms-to-nullify-chinas-missile-supremacy-idUS KBN22I16W

LAM, Willy Wo-Lap. 2015. *Chinese politics in the era of Xi Jinping, renaissance, reform or retrogression?* Abingdon: Routledge.

—— 2019. *The fight for China's future*. Abingdon: Routledge.

LA MAISONNEUVE, Éric de. 2019. *Les défis chinois, la révolution Xi Jinping*. Monaco: Le Rocher.

LAPRÉE, Jérôme, SMAÏLI, Malika, GROSDET, Anthony, *et al.* (dir.). 2018. *Chine/États-Unis: Quelles guerres économiques?* Versailles: VA Press.

LARDY, Nicholas. 2019. *The State strikes back, the end of economic reform in China?* Washington (DC): The Peterson Institute for International Economics.

LAVALLÉE, Guillaume. 2019. China signs deal to 'lease' Tulagi island in the Solomons. *Agence France-Presse*. 17 octobre. URL: https://www.rappler.com/world/asia-pacific/china-leases-pacific-island-solomons-tulagi

Le «scénario cauchemardesque» pour Pékin. 2018. *Les Crises*. 24 novembre. URL: https://www.les-crises.fr/le-scenario-cauchemardesque-pour-pekin-50-millions-dappartements-chinois-sont-vides/

LEBLANC, Claude. 2019. Les États-Unis se préparent au choc de civilisation avec la Chine. *L'Opinion*. 6 mai. URL: https://www.lopinion.fr/edition/international/etats-unis-se-preparent-choc-civilisation-chine-185874

LEE, Dave. 2019. Blocking research with China would 'hurt', Microsoft boss says. *BBC*. October 5. URL: https://www.bbc.com/news/technology-49943037

LEE, Jeong-ho. 2019. US cruise missile test will start a new arms race, says China. *South China Morning Post*. August 20. URL: https://www.scmp.com/news/china/diplomacy/article/3023607/us-cruise-missile-test-will-start-new-arms-race-says-china

LEE, Kai-Fu. 2018. *China, Silicon Valley and the New World Order*. Boston: Houghton Mifflin Harcourt.

—— 2019. *IA, la plus grande mutation de l'histoire*. Paris: Les Arènes.

LENGLET, François. 2010. *La guerre des empires: Chine contre États-Unis*. Paris: Fayard.

Les États-Unis et la Chine se trouvent aujourd'hui au pied d'une guerre froide. 2019. *Newsfront*. 21 novembre. URL: https://fr.news-front.info/2019/11/21/les-etats-unis-et-la-chine-se-trouvent-aujourd-hui-au-pied-d-une-guerre-froide/

L'exercice militaire aérien Chine-Russie, un message aux États-Unis. 2019. *Le Point*. 24 juillet. URL: https://www.lepoint.fr/monde/l-exercice-militaire-aerien-chine-russie-un-message-aux-etats-unis-201326530_24.php

LEYS, Simon. 1976. *Images brisées*. Paris: Robert Laffont.

—— 1978. *Ombres chinoises*. Paris: Robert Laffont.

—— 1983. *La forêt en feu*. Paris: Hermann.

—— 1987. *Les habits neufs du président Mao*. Paris: Ivréa.

—— 2014. *Orwell ou l'horreur de la politique*. Paris: Flammarion.

LIAO, Yiwu. 2019. *Des balles et de l'opium*. Trad. par Marie Holzman. Paris: Globe.

LIN, Yutang. 2019. *La Chine et les Chinois*. Paris: Payot.

LIU, Binyan. 1989. *Le cauchemar des mandarins rouges*. Trad. par Jean-Philippe Béja. Paris: Gallimard.

LIU, John, TIAN, Ying, WHITLEY, Angus, *et al.* 2019. China's father of electric cars says hydrogen is the future. *Bloomberg*. June 12. URL: https://www.bloomberg.com/news/articles/2012/china-s-father-of-electric-cars-thinks-hydrogen-is-the-future

LU, Wenming. 2004. Le rôle croissant de la Chine dans le commerce mondial du bois. *Unasylva* n° 219, vol. 55, p. 27–31. URL: http://www.fao.org/3/y5918f/y5918f06.htm

L'UE et le Japon concoctent une réponse aux «nouvelles routes de la soie» de Pékin. *L'Expansion*. 27 septembre. URL: https://lexpansion.lexpress.fr/actualites/1/actualite-economique/l-ue-et-le-japon-concoctent-une-reponse-auxnouvelles-routes-de-la-soie-de-pekin_2100096.html

MACAES, Bruno. 2018. *Belt and Road: A Chinese World Order.* London: C. Hurst & Co.

MACRON, Emmanuel. 2019. Déclaration sur les défis et priorités de la politique étrangère de la France et de l'Union européenne à Paris, le 27 août. *Vie-publique.* 27 août. URL: https://www.vie-publique.fr/discours/270198-emmanuel-macron-27082019-politique-etrangere>. An English version of the speech is available here: https://lv.ambafrance.org/Ambassadors-conference-Speech-by-M-Emmanuel-Macron-President-of-the-Republic

MAGNUS, George. 2019. *Why Xi's China is in jeopardy.* New Haven: Yale University Press.

MAHLER, Vincent. 2019. Kai-Fu Lee: «L'IA sera plus foudroyante que l'électricité». *Le Point.* 29 août. URL: https://www.pressreader.com/france/le-point/2019 0829/281569472393281

MARTIN, Claude. 2018. *La diplomatie n'est pas un dîner de gala.* La Tour d'Aigues: l'Aube.

MARTIN, Peter, HAN, Miao, LI, Dandan, TIAN, Ying. 2019. China committed to peace despite challenges, vice president says. *Bloomberg.* November 20. URL: https://www.bloomberg.com/news/articles/2011/china-s-vice-president-wang-qishan-to-address-economic-forum

MCGREGOR, Richard. 2010. *The Party: The secret world of China's communist rulers.* New York: Harper Reed. 2012.

MCMAHON, Dinny. 2019. *China's Great Wall of debt: Shadow banks, ghost cities, massive loans and the end of the Chinese miracle.* London: Abacus.

Merkel calls for Europe to agree on China 5G policy. 2019. *Reuters.* November 27. URL: https://www.reuters.com/article/germany-china-merkel/merkel-calls-for-europe-to-agree-on-china-5g-policy-idUSS8N2860B7

MEUDEC, Olivia. 2017. La Chine, talon d'Achille de l'Union européenne. *Asia focus (IRIS)* n° 32. URL: https://www.iris-france.org/observatoires/asia-focus/11/

MEYER, Claude. 2018. *L'Occident face à la renaissance de la Chine.* Paris: Odile Jacob.

MINZNER, Carl. 2018. *End of an era, how China's authoritarian revival is undermining its rise.* Oxford: Oxford University Press.

MULLEN, Jethro and STEVENS, Andrew. 2016. Billionaire: Chinese real estate is 'biggest bubble in history'. *CNN.* September 29. URL: https://money.cnn.com/2016/09/28/investing/china-wang-jianlin-real-estate-bubble/

MUNDA, Constant. 2019. China takes up 87 pc of Kenya Interest payment. *Kenyan Tribune.* September 25. URL: https://www.kenyantribune.com/china-takes-up-87pc-of-kenya-interest-payment/

NASA wants international partners to go to Moon too. 2019. *Agence France-Presse.* October 22.

NAVARRO, Peter, AUTRY, Greg. 2011. *Death by China: Confronting the dragon, a global call to action*. London: FT Pearson.

NAVARRO, Peter, CHANG, Gordon G. 2015. *Crouching tiger: What China's militarism means for the world*. New York: Prometheus Books.

NIQUET, Valérie. 2017. *La puissance chinoise, un géant fragile?* Paris: Tallandier.

ONG, Russell. 2013. *China's strategic competition with the United States*. Abingdon: Routledge.

ORWELL, George. *1949*. 1984.

OSNOS, Evan. 2015. *Age of ambitions: Chasing fortune, truth and faith in the new China*. London: The Bodley Head.

PAQUET, Philippe. 2004. *L'ABCédaire de la Chine*. Arles: Philippe Picquier.

—— 2010. *Madame Chiang Kai-shek, un siècle d'histoire de la Chine*. Paris: Gallimard.

—— 2016. *Simon Leys, navigateur entre les mondes*. Paris: Gallimard.

PASQUALINI, Jean. 1975. *Prisonnier de Mao; sept ans dans un camp de travail en Chine*. Paris: Gallimard.

PEI, Minxin. 2016. *China's crony capitalism; the dynamics of regime decay*. Cambridge (Ma): Harvard University Press.

—— 2019. China's Communist Party is looking at the beginning of the end of one-party rule. *South China Morning Post*. September 22. URL: https://www.scmp.com/comment/opinion/article/3029809/chinas-communist-party-looking-beginning-end-one-party-rule

PENDLETON, John. 2019. Army readiness: progress and challenges in rebuilding personnel, equipping and training. US Government Accountability Office. February 6. URL: https://www.gao.gov/assets/700/697646.pdf

Pew Research Center. 2020. Unfavorable Views of China Reach Historic Highs in Many Countries. October. https://www.pewresearch.org/global/2020/10/06/unfavorable-views-of-china-reach-historic-highs-in-many-countries/

PEYREFITTE, Alain. 1973. *Quand la Chine s'éveillera… le monde tremblera*. Paris: Fayard.

PILLSBURY, Michael. 2016. *The hundred-year marathon: China's secret strategy to replace America as the global superpower*. New York: Saint Martin's Griffin.

PITRON, Guillaume. 2018. *La guerre des métaux rares*. Paris: LLL.

POLO, Marco. 1298. *Le Devisement du monde*.

POMPEO, Mike. 2019. The China challenge. Lecture, Hudson Institute, New York City, NY, October 30. URL: https://uy.usembassy.gov/michael-r-pompeo-at-the-hudson-institutes-herman-kahn-award-gala/

PUEL, Caroline. 2013. *Les Trente Glorieuses chinoises*. Paris: Tempus.

Putin says accepts U.S. is sole superpower, dilutes Trump praise. 2016. *Reuters*. June 17. URL: https://www.reuters.com/article/us-russia-forum-putin-usa-idUSKCN0Z31G4

QIAO, Long. 2019. China's Party Plenum gets behind president at 'complicated' time. *Radio Free Asia*. October 31. URL: https://www.rfa.org/english/news/china/plenum-10312019135440.html

Questions à Jean-Paul Tchang. 2019. Résumé de «L'Invité de 6 h 20» sur France Inter le 21 mars 2019, entretien avec Mathilde Munos. *Pileface*. URL: http://www.pileface.com/sollers/spip.php?article2087

RAJAH, Roland, DAYANT, Alexandre, PRYKE, Jonathan. 2019. Debt diplomacy in the Pacific. October 21. Sydney: *Lowy Institute*. URL: https://www.lowyinstitute.org/publications/ocean-debt-belt-and-road-and-debt-diplomacy-pacific

REICHLIN, Catherine. 2019. L'ambiguïté de la Chine en matière de dette d'entreprise. *Agefi*. 17 juillet. URL: https://www.agefi.com/home/news/detail-ageficom/edition/online/article/obligataire-plus-de-40-milliards-de-dollars-de-dette-de-57-societes-chinoises-avec-echeance-2019-sont-sous-pression-489144.html

REID, David. 2019. Boeing values China's aircraft business at almost $3 trillion over the next two decades. *CNBC*. September 17. URL: https://www.cnbc.com/2019/09/17/boeing-says-china-needs-to-spend-almost-3-trillion-on-new-planes.html

RICCI, Joël. 2019. Un troisième C919 réussit son vol test. *Air Journal*. 30 décembre. URL: https://www.air-journal.fr/2010-un-troisieme-c919-reussit-son-voltest-5209173.html

RINGEN, Stein. 2016. *The perfect dictatorship: China in the 21st century*. Hong Kong: HKU Press.

ROBERT, Philippine. 2018. Chine: son incroyable percée dans les technologies d'avenir. *Capital*. 25 juin. URL: https://www.capital.fr/economie-politique/chine-son-incroyable-percee-dans-les-technologies-davenir-1294784

ROCCA, Jean-Louis. 2010. *Une sociologie de la Chine*. Paris: La Découverte.

ROMEI, Valentina, REED, John. 2019. The Asian century is set to begin. *Financial Times*. March 26. URL: https://www.ft.com/content/520cb6f951e9-a5ab-ff8ef2b976c7

ROSECRANCE, Richard. 1986. *The rise of the trading state: Commerce in the modern world*. New York: Basic Books.

ROSECRANCE, Richard, GUOLIANG, Gu. 2009. *Power and restraint: A shared vision for the U.S.-China relationship*. New York: Public Affairs.

ROSECRANCE, Richard, MILLER, Steven E. 2015. *The next great war, the roots of World War I and the risk of U.S.-China conflict*. Cambridge (Ma): MIT Press.

Russia-China military provocations cloak diverging interests in Central Asia. 2019. *Caravanserai*. July 26. URL: https://central.asia-news.com/en_GB/articles/cnmi_ca/features/2019/07/26/feature-02

Russia helping China to create early missile warning system, says Putin. 2019. *TASS*. October 3. URL: https://tass.com/defense/1081383

SAMAMA, Pascal. 2019. Pour Elon Musk, l'intelligence artificielle menace plus que jamais l'humanité. *BFMTV*. 29 août. URL: https://www.bfmtv.com/tech/pour-elon-musk-l-intelligence-artificielle-menace-plus-que-jamais-l-humanite_AN-2019 08290053.html

SANCHEZ MANZANARO Sofia, and Abellan-Matamoros. 2019. What are rare earth elements and why are they so important in the US-China trade war? Euronews. August 16. URL: https://www.euronews.com/2019/08/15/what-are-rare-earth-elements-and-why-are-they-so-important-in-the-us-china-trade-war

SHAMBAUGH, David. 2019. The challenges China faces in securing global dominance. Speech given to the Hong Kong Foreign Correspondents' Club on October 22. URL: https://www.fcchk.org/the-challenges-china-faces-in-securing-global-dominance

SHEARER, Christine, YU, Aiqun, NACE, Ted. 2019. Out of step: China is driving the continued growth of the global coal fleet. *Global Energy Monitor*. November. URL: https://endcoal.org/2019/11/new-report-out-of-step-china-is-driving-the-continued-growth-of-the-global-coal-fleet/

SHEEHAN, Matt. 2019. *The Transpacific experiment; How China and California collaborate and compete for our future.* Berkeley: Counterpoint Press.

SHEPARDSON, David, HORWITZ, Josh. 2019. US expands blacklist to include China's top AI startups ahead of trade talks. *Reuters*. October 7. URL: https://fr.reuters.com/article/asia/idUSKBN1WM25M

SCHUBERT, Gunter. 2003. La démocratie peut-elle coexister avec le Parti unique? *Perspectives chinoises*, n° 75, janvier-février, p. 16–28. URL: https://www.persee.fr/doc/perch_102013_2003_num_75_1_2917

SIDANE, Victor. 1980. *Le printemps de Pékin.* Paris: Gallimard.

SONG, Yongyi. 2009. *Les massacres de la Révolution culturelle.* Paris: Gallimard.

SUN, Haoran, ZHAO, Yusha. 2019. Most cyber attacks from the US: Report. *Global Times*. June 10. URL: http://www.globaltimes.cn/content/1153777.shtml

TANG, Zhe. 2019. XI Jinping portraits replace catholic symbols in churches. *Bitter Winter*. November 21. URL: https://bitterwinter.org/xi-jinping-portraits-replace-catholic-symbols/

TANGUY, Vincent. 2017. Poutine pense dominer le monde en maîtrisant l'intelligence artificielle. *Sciences et avenir*. 5 septembre. URL: https://www.sciencesetavenir.fr/high-tech/intelligence-artificielle/poutine-pense-dominer-le-monde-en-maitrisant-l-intelligence-artificielle_116062

TELLIER, Maxime. 2019. L'intelligence artificielle au service des ambitions de la Chine. *France culture*. 29 août. URL: https://www.franceculture.fr/geopolitique/lintelligence-artificielle-au-service-des-ambitions-de-la-chine

TESTARD, Hubert. 2019a. Comment la Chine est revenue au premier plan. *Asialyst*. 28 septembre. URL: https://asialyst.com/fr/2019/09/28/comment-chine-revenue-premier-plan/

—— 2019b. 70 ans de la Chine populaire: l'affirmation d'un contre-modèle. *Asialyst*. 30 septembre. URL: https://asialyst.com/fr/2019/09/30/chine-populaire-70-ans-affirmation-contre-modele/

THUCYDIDE. *La guerre du Péloponnèse.*

The Chinese consumer in 2030. 2016. *The Economist Intelligence Unit.* November 2. URL: http://country.eiu.com/article.aspx?articleid=1584774142

Time to care: Unpaid and underpaid care work and the global inequality crisis. 2020. *Oxfam.* January. URL: https://www.oxfam.org/en/research/time-care

TOCQUEVILLE, Alexis de. 2019 [1835]. *De la démocratie en Amérique, vol. 2.* Paris: Flammarion.

TOUZANI, Samir. 2018. La Chine veut définitivement enterrer le contrôle des naissances. *Les Échos.* 28 août. URL: https://www.lesechos.fr/monde/chine/la-chine-veut-definitivement-enterrer-le-controle-des-naissances-137497

TOWNSHEND, Ashley, THOMAS-NOONE, Brendan, STEWARD, Matilda. 2019. Averting crisis: American strategy, military spending and collective defence in the Indo-Pacific. Sydney: United States Studies Centre. August 19. URL: https://www.ussc.edu.au/analysis/averting-crisis-american-strategy-military-spending-and-collective-defence-in-the-indo-pacific

Trump ordonne aux entreprises américaines de quitter la Chine. 2019. *La Tribune.* 23 août. URL: https://www.latribune.fr/economie/international/trump-ordonne-aux-entreprises-americaines-de-quitter-la-chine-826309.html

Un Bol de nids d'hirondelles ne fait pas le printemps de Pékin. 1980. Paris: Christian Bourgois.

United Nations. 2019. Perspectives de la population mondiale, communiqué de presse, 17 juin. URL: https://population.un.org/wpp/Publications/Files/WPP2019_PressRelease_FR.pdf

VAVASSEUR, Xavier. 2020. South Korea to double down on F-35 and procure STOVL Variant for LPX-II. *Naval News.* September 4. URL: https://www.navalnews.com/naval-news/2020/09/south-korea-to-double-down-on-f-35-and-procure-stovl-variant-for-lpx-ii/

VILLAIN, Jacques. s.d. Les États-Unis, puissance dominante. *Encyclopédia universalis.* URL: https://www.universalis.fr/encyclopedie/espace-conquete-de-l-la-militarisation-de-l-espace/

VINCENT, Danny. 2019. How China plans to lead the computer chip industry. *BBC.* November 19. URL: https://www.bbc.com/news/business-50287485

WALT, Stephen. 2006. *Taming the American power: The global response to US primacy.* New York: Norton.

WANG, Alain. 2018. *Les Chinois*. Paris: Tallandier.

WANG, Kelly. 2019. China's quest for clean, limitless energy heats up. *Agence France-Presse*, April 29.

WANG, Gungwu. 2019. *China reconnects, joining a deep-rooted past to a New World Order*. Singapore: World Scientific.

WARD, Jonathan D.T. 2019. *China's vision of victory*. Fayetteville (NC): Atlas Publishing.

'We don't steal': China slams FBI's intellectual, property theft accusation. 2019. *CGTN*. July 24. URL: https://news.cgtn.com/news/2014/-We-don-t-steal-China-slams-FBI-s-intelligence-theft-remarks-IAH13IpN7O/index.html

Why China's debt defaults look set to pick up again, 2019. *Bloomberg*. July 18. URL: https://www.bloomberg.com/professional/blog/chinas-debt-defaults-look-set-pick/

WOODWARD, Jude. 2017. *US vs China, Asia's new Cold War?* Manchester: Manchester University Press.

World Bank. 2019. China's experience with high speed rail offers lessons for other countries. July 8. URL: https://www.worldbank.org/en/news/press-release/2019/07/08/chinas-experience-with-high-speed-rail-offers-lessons-for-other-countries

WRIGHT, Logan and FENG, Allen. 2020. COVID-19 and China's household debt dilemma. *Rhodium Group*. May 12. URL: https://rhg.com/research/china-household-debt/

WU, Harry. 1999. *Le goulag chinois*. Paris: Dagorno.

Xi Jinping warns attempts to divide China will end in 'shattered bones'. 2019. *Reuters*. October 13. URL: https://fr.reuters.com/article/us-china-politics-xi-idUSK BN1WS07W

XU, Muyu, STANWAY, David. 2019. China's ocean waste surges 27% in 2018. *Reuters*. October 29. URL: https://www.reuters.com/article/us-china-pollution-oceans/chinasocean-waste-surges-27-in-2018-ministry-idUSKBN1X80FL

YANG, Jishen. 2012. *Stèles, la grande famine, 1959–1962*. Paris: Seuil.

ZAUGG, Julie. 2019. L'Italie est à la botte de Pékin. *Le Temps*. 21 mars. URL: https://www.letemps.ch/economie/litalie-botte-pekin

ZHANG, Weiwei. 2016. *The China horizon: Glory and dream of a civilizational state*. Hackensack (NJ): World Century.

ZHANG, Zhulin. 2019. En Chine, le nombre de naissances est en très nette diminution. *Courrier international*. 2 janvier. URL: https://www.courrierinternational.com/revue-de-presse/en-chine-le-nombre-de-naissances-est-en-tres-nette-diminution

ZHEN, Liu, NG, Teddy. 2019. Chinese President Xi Jinping warns of disaster if one civilisation imposes its will on another. *South China Morning Post.* May 15. URL: https://www.scmp.com/news/china/diplomacy/article/3010287/cultural-superiority-stupid-and-disastrous-chinese-president

ZWEIG, David, HAO, Yufan. 2016. *Sino-U.S. energy triangles: Resource diplomacy under hegemony.* Abingdon: Routledge.

Publications by the Author

Le Dragon et la Souris (with Lawrence MacDonald), Christian Bourgois, 1987.

Tibet mort ou vif, Gallimard, 1990, 1991; Folio Actuel, 1993. Préface d'Élisabeth Badinter. Translated into five languages. Updated and expanded edition published in March 2019. Winner of Alexandra David-Néel Prize in 1990.

Le Japon achète le monde, Seuil, 1991 (Translated into Chinese).

Tibet, des journalistes témoignent (with Jean-Paul Ribes and Guy Privat), L'Harmattan, 1992.

Tibet, un autre monde (with Robert Dompnier), Olizane, 1993.

Cabu au Japon (with Cabu), Seuil, 1993 (Translated into Chinese).

Au Tibet avec Tintin, collectif, Casterman, 1994.

Le choc Europe-Asie, Seuil, 1998.

Asie, les nouvelles règles du jeu, collectif, Philippe Picquier, 1999.

Cabu en Chine (with Cabu), Seuil, 2000 (Translated into Chinese).

Le Japon, la fin d'une économie (with Anne Garrigue), Gallimard/Le Monde, 2000.

Cabu en Inde (with Cabu), Seuil, 2002 (Translated into Chinese).

Pontgibaud et son canton, Alan Sutton, 2003.

Volcans d'Auvergne: les montagnes et les hommes, Alan Sutton, 2003.

Les Châteaux d'Auvergne, Alan Sutton, 2004.

Villes d'eaux en Auvergne, Alan Sutton, 2006.

Chirac, pile et face (with Thierry Dussard), Hoebeke, 2007.

La Saga Michelin, Seuil, 2008.

Chine, 30 ans de photographies de l'Agence France-Presse, Philippe Picquier, 2008.

Quand la Chine achète le monde, Philippe Picquier, 2018. Turgot 2019 Special Prize. Paperback edition, 2019.